GW00702269

Images of Life

-

In Rhyme

– DENNIS SHRUBSHALL –

An environmentally friendly book printed and bound in England
by www.printondemand-worldwide.com

Mixed Sources
Product group from well-managed
forests, and other controlled sources
www.fsc.org Cert no. TT-COC-002641
© 1996 Forest Stewardship Council

FSC

PEFC Certified
This product is
from sustainably
managed forests
and controlled
sources
www.pefc.org
PEFC/16-33-416

This book is made entirely of chain-of-custody materials

www.fast-print.net/store.php

Images of Life – In Rhyme
Copyright © Dennis Shrubshall 2012

ISBN 978-178035-458-3

First published 2012 by
FASTPRINT PUBLISHING
Peterborough, England.

Foreword

Foreword

"Images of Life in Rhyme" by Dennis Shrubshall is a fascinating collection of poetry. Dennis manages over and over to capture the realities of ordinary life in his verse which we can all relate to and he manages to put into words so many of our own thoughts and emotions.

Dennis is an uncomplicated man of many parts he has clear views of right and wrong and works hard at all that he does whether that be his business or in his work for bowls. He is a giver and not a taker and the fact that he will donate profits from this book to the Haven Hospice for Children & Adults is evidence of his commitment to the community.

This is a book of poetry for everyone. It is not for reading but for dipping into at random for there are many treasures to be found in his work. If you enjoyed his first work "A Tapestry of Verse" then this is a must read.

David MG.

Biography

Born in Forest Gate in the East End of London in 1933, the fourth child in a Family of six. Childhood spent through the WW2 years and then on to Grammar School until 1948.

Started work as a Railway clerk in London and then into the RAF in 1952 as a Radar Operator for 2 years. Since then has spent 58 years in the Building Trade as a Master Builder. Married 1957 and has 2 Daughters and 5 Grand children and 4 great grand children. Played Bowls for 40 years including representing Essex over 100 times. First wrote poetry in 1973 but more prolifically in the last 5 years with the advent of a word processor Now semi retired living in the house he built 40 years ago in Benfleet, Essex. He is now "Shrubby the Essex Bard"

This Volume if dedicated to my 2 daughters
Wendy Janice Fowler & Carole Anne Earl
and both of their families
for their continued support in my writing

In an English Country Garden

As I sat alone in a quiet room
I gazed from the window
And saw Flowers bloom
To form a floral picture there
Of a typical English Garden
The lawn now green from a Winter rest
Where Daffodils and Jonquils show best
Amongst Snowdrops and Tulips
In a wonderful hue
Here and there some Marigolds too
Budding Roses standing bold
Waiting their outer leaves to unfold
And display the beauty hidden there
A sign of the loving Gardener's care
Keeping them free from bugs and mites
That seem to fill the air
Which now is filled with a fragrant scent
Is this what Mother Nature meant
Or was it merely heaven sent
To an English Country Garden
The lawn is mowed to perfection
Not a weed nor clover is seen
Even the edges of the flower beds
Trimmed with a blade so keen
Shredded bark in abundance
Strewn on the Rose beds with care
In a concentrated effort to assure

No weeds are growing there
There's a sign of the Peonies nudging through
After their winter rest
Always hoping for a windless June
So they can look their best
Here and there among the beds
Fuchsias Blues & Mauves & Reds
Hoping their variegated heads
Will set up a radiant glow
But the Flower that is my favorite
From South Africa it came
Is the lovely Osteosternum
Or an African Daisy by another name
But I mustn't forget the stately trees
That afford the garden some shade
The Flowering Cherry, Apple and Pear
Their blossom and fruit well displayed
And they are also haven to our feathered friends
Be it Summer Winter or Spring
And as you casually stroll in the Garden
Hear the lovely creatures sing
All a part of Natures Rich Tapestry
Throughout the hours when it's light
But then comes the Shadow of Eventide
Followed by the silence of the night.

Dennis Shrubshall   12th August 2008

Is Summer Really here

The weather's changed, is Summer here
Welcomed by one and all
After a long and bitter Winter
So cold beyond recall
Spring was so long arriving
The telltale signs were late
No sign of any new plant life
Too cold for them to germinate
But now there's a hint to Summertime
A friendly warmth is in the air
Bloom on the flowers and blossom on the trees
Which makes us all aware
Apprehensive of what the Summer might bring
Ever conscious of Season's past
Will we be scorched from the heat of the Sun
Or cold and wet from rain and a chill wind blast
Trees are in full leaf now
Blossom's gone but the fruits are set
Hoping for a blight free Summer
Enhancing the fruit harvest we may get
Resting in the shade of the trees
The well filled flower beds
The Roses are healthy and now in bud
And the flowers showing their variegated coloured heads
The Peonies rise majestically in Scarlet, White and Pink
As their blooms open so pristine
But not for long is their beauty on view

Blown by the wind and a carpet of blossom petals are seen
Hydrangeas are looking strong now, Agapanthus too
Stems waiting for their blossoms to appear
With their Mauve, Blue, Pink and White colours
Adorning the beds year after year
The Roses are starting to open there buds
The first Rose of Summer you'll hear some folks say
But 'fore long the beds are resplendent in Blossom
Creating a wonderful display
Chrysanthemums, Fuchsias and Gladioli too
All growing now in the warmth of the Summer Sun
Creating beauty for the eye of the beholder
Once again Mother Nature's Flower Show has begun

Dennis Shrubshall   28th May 2010

No Hiding Place

When everything is going wrong
Do you sit and contemplate
What has caused this turbulence
To make you so irate
Is it the intolerance
Of others near and far
Unwittingly to upset your life
Without reasons particular
So stand your ground my friend
No need to build a wall
As everything will turn out right
As from their haughty perch they fall
So many times it's proven
If behind four walls you hide
How can your friends contact you
When you need them by your side
To carry on from day to day
Enjoying life to the full
At times it strains your resources
Where from, the strength, you'll pull
Energy and understanding
Equilibrium returns to your door
And you can carry on your life
Happy and carefree as before.

Dennis Shrubshall   9th February 2009

9

Penny for your thoughts

Sit if you will and close your eyes
And set yourself an awesome task
Erase all the worries that beset you
And I know that's a great deal to ask
Now you're sitting with a mind that is clear
So now the next thing to do
Bring back for a moment but one at a time
All the things that are troubling you
If you feel at some point that you need a third party
I'm sure a loved one's not too far away
With a shoulder to lean on and a listening ear
To get troubles sorted today
For I know it's not easy, from experience
To cope with what you're going through
When you feel that you've come to the end of your tether
But love and friendship will pull you through
But you must share your troubles they're too much to
keep
And then the solutions may start
So look to your friends and your Family
To take the worry and strain and lift the load from your
heart
Let your Mum live her life and help where you can
Though at times with a heart that is breaking
For it's not easy to hide your emotions
But a way out is not there for the taking
So dry your tears and hold your head up high

And be proud that you do what you can
To try to achieve the impossible dream
Not easy to create a master plan
Now open your eyes on this bright new world
For you've just swept all the cobwebs away
Look forward to a bright new tomorrow
And goodbye to a sad yesterday.

Dennis Shrubshall   3rd November 2010

Loving Embrace

Love is defined in so many ways
Sometimes hard to understand
It maybe just a look from across the room
Or a meaningful wave of the hand
As many feel that love is just for the young
But that is a myth I'm sure
For love is within everybody in some form
From life until death or evermore
But picture if you will the image
Of two young persons in love
Happy with their life in every form
As tho' floating on clouds up above
But then out of the blue the realism
That parents they are likely to be
Another step on the road of life
Towards maturity
And then there are anxious moments
Will it be a young girl or a boy
Though it matter not to most couples
As their worlds will now fill with joy
And now through this happy union
The young mother is able to give birth
And fulfil their love with a child of their own
More precious than Gold in worth
So love can be fulfilled in many different ways
Perhaps help others when they are in need
For there are many less fortunate in life

Where fate has barred there way to succeed
And if you picture an infant in a Mother's arms
Cocooned in her loving care to be able to live
So think hard of those that you know are in need
And embrace them with all the love you can give.

Dennis Shrubshall   4th January 2011

Fatima

This story started some time ago
On an Island not far away
New Guinea in the Pacific Ocean
Where some Australians visit or stay
Fatima was the destination
For Kathy at this time
When she was working there with Missionaries
Where happiness reigned sublime
The party consisted of Priests and Nuns
And the missionaries too
Living together in unison
As Christian parties do
The accomodation was very basic
Inflatable beds on the floor
Living the life of the Natives
No luxuries were in store
There were no windows but holes in the walls
In what was little more than a hut
But it did posses a door of sorts
Which residents were able to shut
All the young ladies together
For Kathy all was going fine
They all decided to celebrate
With some food and the odd glass of wine
And then it was back to their billet
They walked as best they could
With everything dark around them

And a torch which did little good
They made their way in single file
Down a goat track or something such
With bush a foliage around them
Their steps couldn't vary much
Then Kathy heard a noise at her side
She jumped forward and all the other girls stumbled and
fell
Some screamed and some nearly cried
But all the noise had woken the bush life
Their cries could be heard all around
And then it seemed as if by magic
There wasn't a single sound
They were settled back in their billet now
An Kathy looked towards the top of the door
Was distracted by talking and laughter
And then looked back once more
But this time on top of the door the big head of a Snake
The biggest Kathy had ever seen
And eyes that looked at her as if to say
Stay there for me my little queen
Tho petrified Kathy tried to shout a warning
Then "SNAKE SNAKE" she shouted but in vain
For the other girls took no notice
They thought she was kidding again
By this time the snake was on the floor now
And they finally heeded | Kathy's cries
As they were faced with huge 10ft snake
With a big head and mesmerising eyes
Then Kathy just jumped through the window
With all the others to land on the scrub beneath
When one of the older Nuns murmured
I'm going back in there it's not having my teeth
The Nun then dived back & returned with her teeth in the
glass
Put teeth in and threw the glass at the snakes head
They gathered and waited till they were all together
And off down the path they all fled
By now the men ran towards them
To investigate the cause of the noise
But by now the snake has made it's way through the door
To find which escape route it deploys
A man then said "Girls don't be afraid of that

15

You've made such a silly mistake"
That little fella won't hurt you
It's only a baby | Carpet Snake

Dennis Shrubshall   2nd December 2011

Ruins on the Moor

The moor looked so desolate
Uninviting to me
But this was the challenge
I would face with impunity
To walk the path that very few trod
Looking for conquests new
Was there some danger lurking there
Beyond the Horizon so blue
The Sun was rising there in the East
A golden halo spreading fast
Tho' I knew that during my day long trek
This beautiful weather might not last
Mile after mile I strode along
Hoping directions were right
To study the ancient ruins
And get back to my lodging by night
All of a sudden came into view
A sight which to me was so rare
This wonderful relic of a bygone age
Gracefully standing there
And as I approached this ageing fortress
Or perhaps an Abbey of days gone by
And there through the crumbling masonry
Some portals I did espy
Or were they the remains that surrounded
The exit or entry therein
This was the start of my challenge

Where my adventure would begin
The trees drew themselves in a mantle
As tho' to shelter this magical scene
For grass had replaced the floors of stone
Creating tranquility serene
Curiosity has descended
Upon my furrowed brow
Shall I stay and see this scene by night
Or shall I leave right now
But it would be such a pity to go
For the dusk was Oh! so near
Would this be a treat in the moonlight
Minute sounds so very clear
A couple of Rabbits go scurrying by
The last of the song birds sing
As I look to what may have been a belfry
Will I hear those ancient bells ring
The strangest thoughts all come to mind
As I stroll there all alone
Will I see the ghosts of a thousand years
As their fates they all bemoan
The time is passing quickly
Was that an old hinge I heard squeak
Will I see a ghostly hooded figure walk by
And in some bygone language speak
The Moon is full in the Heavens now
In a perfectly cloudless sky
Like a spotlight on this Crumbling ruin
Can I imagine if I try
To think of this monument in infancy
With horsemen riding by
Perhaps knights in shining armour
And damsels in distress as well
Apparently this is how it happened then
Or that is how I've heard folks tell
The dawn is coming up now
And I'm happy that I stayed
To see the ruins in different aspects
Ancient memories displayed
So it's time for me to leave now
And make the return journey back home
walking across that desolate moor
Going home alone

When I could write a journal
On this fascinating day
A journey back to yesteryear
Perfect in every way.

Dennis Shrubshall   16th September 2008

The Naked Run

My thoughts go back to a Sunday morn
Oh! so many years ago
When recollections started
And past memories started to flow
To a time when I was a Special Police Officer
To prevent crime was my main aim
As a WPC in uniform
And part of the local crimebusters I became
We drove along my colleague and I
In a Patrol car for all to see
When a call came over the Radio
And the recipient was me
The crime we were told was Graffitti
On a "wheelie" bin tho' written quite neatly
Insulting remarks about the owner's Son
Puzzling the inhabitants completely
So out came the note-book and details we noted
All standard questions to victims we posed
In an effort to identify the offender
And in Court their crimes be disclosed
But then came another call on the Radio
Of another similar offence not far away
So off we sped in the Patrol car
To see what the latest victims had to say
Surprise was obvious on both of our faces
As we surveyed this new scene
For believe it or not it had all the same hallmarks

Of the address where we had just been
Insults once more against the lad of the house
On Garden Furniture in emulsion white
Impeccably written without grammatical error
Who could be this demon of the night
And so once again the questions we asked
The various notes we started to make
For if this should come to Court at some time
The Defence would welcome any mistake
Then lo and behold yet another Radio call
Reporting a third and similar crime
Everything similar except for one thing
A neighbour witnessed the event this time
Who heard a noise and saw a naked man
Run away with a brush and paint tin in his hand
And I admit at that time we were baffled
The offenders motive difficult to understand
We spotted and followed a trail of paint spots
This was the main clue we had found
And when we came to an area of grass
It was there that our offender went to ground
So then it was down to deduction work
To see if a link we could find
For this was more than a childish prank
A revenge filled attack from a disturbed mind
The lads we found out were Boy Scouts all three
And a young Leader they relentlessly teased
And this was his way of displaying to them all
That he was a little more than displeased
And then with all this accomplished
The offenders name we now knew
So we ended out shift and passed on the "info"
For another team to pursue
They visited his house the following day
Then outlined the crime when admitted
May lead to a mandatory visit to Court
Where he may be found guilty or acquitted
But the case was settled there by the Constables
And if help from the Doctor he retract
They would have no other alternative
To be sectioned under the Mental Health Act .

Dennis Shrubshall   15th November 2009

21

The Professional Soldier

If you were asked a thousand questions
Or maybe even more
About your views on conflict
In any given theatre War
Do you think that it is possible
That given thought, you might
Agree that War is justified
And send our Army to fight
For this must be the situation
That a Government of the day must face
When asked for help from across the World
So that from War with Peace they may replace
For although we live in a small Island
Our Military Men are measured with high esteem
They may be asked to quell a "coups d'etat, in some far
flung land
No matter how difficult the task may seem
They fought in the hills of Korea
And in the jungles of Borneo and Malaya too
Not forgetting their fight in the Falkland Islands
And the IRA in Ireland to pursue
Although things have changed with the passing of time
And mostly in the forms of transport they use
No longer do they sit aboard a troopship for weeks
As though on an extended holiday cruise
For they knew that after weeks of inactivity
That when on foreign soil they land

They had to return to fighting fitness, at the double
To get on the with the job in hand
But today the mode of travel is much quicker
As they walk aboard a large Transporter plane
And fly to that far off destination, where
In 24 hours they are in action again
Although it is said in War there is only one winner
And we know the "Grim Reaper " is his name
If you asked the average British Soldier, what he thinks
Most would answer " We'll do our job just the same"
For tho' the years come and go a Soldier's job will never
change
As with many Family tradition comes to the fore
And they long to wear the Regimental Uniform of their kin
Then adjust to the changing patterns and weapons of War
For these are the men who choose to fight
As Professional Soldiers they must
So as they serve for the Flag , their Country and their
Queen
In the knowledge of Great Britain's utmost trust.

Dennis Shrubshall   1st June 2009

Radio Times

Time to reflect on yesteryear
To think of days long gone
As you reclined in comfort in the garden
And for company had the Radio on
You thought of the days as a young girl
When you ran and skipped with ease
On the way for a meeting in the Park with your friends
To enjoy yourselves in any way you please
There were swings and even a roundabout
Which you could all jump on and ride
As you sit and contemplate what to do next
Perhaps come down backwards on the slide
Though childhood at the time passed so slowly, so it
seemed
But on reflection those days went so fast
And you realised your schooldays were over
When your final Exams you had passed
And now into a young lady you had grown
Perhaps with tears that mixed with laughter
It was time for you to earn a living on your own
To succeed in life you have to be a grafter
You knew it wouldn't be too easy
In that great big world out there to find
A career that would give you most security
And to live your life with peace of mind
But if you were asked to look back, in life
Is there something you would choose to change

Or do you merely accept life as it is
And nothing wish to re-arrange
For life is a long and winding road
And wisdom comes with age
Instead of growing older, as you think
In your book of life you've written another page
And now you've come back to the present day
Is there somewhere you'd like to go
Or are you content to sit in the Garden
And listen to your Radio.

Dennis Shrubshall   13th July 2009

" *Keisser* "

It's nice to just sit and think of a pet
And many folk do just that
Would they like horses or rabbits
Or maybe a Dog or a cat
But the person I know that comes to mind
Although we have never met
Have on many occasions discussed
The ownership of a Family pet
The person in mind was her Son in this case
With thoughts of a 30th Birthday gift
Of a dog of which he'd be proud
And maybe his inhibitions lift
I think Mum had in mind a Man's dog
Maybe powerful and strong
Able to cope with life as a pet
Or guardian if necessity came along
A Rottweiller Puppy was what they chose
Sometimes a "Rottie" for short
Both now entering a learning curve
As the Puppy obedience was taught
He was aptly named as "Keisser"
For of German breed was he
Working and "herding" dogs of the past
Now coping as Pets and Security
He settled in well in his new home
Becoming a companion and friend
To a young and appreciative owner

And the boundaries were without end
But on some occasions when Keisser's lonely
Around to   Mum's house he would go
To keep each other company through the night
Once again the friendship would show
He would demonstrate the art of a Family pet
Walk about with perfect ease
Then go the window and bark at passers by
As though it was Mum he had to please
A Rottweiller can be playful and a friend to children
And attention and affection they may seek
But left all alone or ill treated
Havoc and destruction they can wreak
But" Keisser" is admired by many
He's gentle and playful with some
But he's always enthusiastic when it's time once again
To spend another night and day with Mum

Dennis Shrubshall   10th February 2012

Deprived of Sleep

Another busy day is left behind
As home from the Office I travel
Back to the comfort of my home
Where all my thoughts I can un-ravel
As I sit in the chair , switch on the T V
Is there anything of interest there
And if the answer is in the negative
For entertainment I'll look elsewhere
So it's now that I go to the bookcase
As up and down the shelves I look
Browsing through the volumes there
To perhaps find a suitable book
But after reading a little while
My concentration seems to be gone
So it's now time to use the last option
And turn my computer on
I quickly check through my emails
Nothing of interest there
So I then go into a Chat room
And sit further back in my swivel chair
The room has a worldwide attraction
Lots of Nations represented there
With Members airing their views and worries
And sometimes laughter will fill the air
As I sit and smile with a glass of wine in my hand
For sometimes the repartee is quite smart
But words can be misinterpreted

And that's where bad feelings can start
But it's one of those nights
When enough I enough
So I logged out as I said my goodbyes
Then looked at the clock on the mantelshelf
And thought "Goodness me how quickly time flies"
So it's time for a nightcap and off up to bed
To undress then under the Duvet I creep
I lay on my side with head on the pillow
And instead of drifting off to sleep
My mind is starting to recall events of the day
Did my computer misunderstand me
Were there Gremlins on the inside
Or did I repeatedly hit the wrong key
Did I really upset one of my colleagues
With those few words spoken in jest
Or was she imitating a grimace
As an actress it was what she did best
I've started to think of my holidays
And my eyes are closing as I lay there alone
Drifting off into a dream world
When rudely awoken by the sound of the phone
So I sat up and confusedly answered
What turned out to be a "wrong call"
Replaced the receiver turned over and lay down
Wondering if tonight I will ever sleep at all
Then pulled the Duvet right over my head
And laid there for what seemed like hours
Hoping to drift off into a beautiful sleep
Perhaps dream of others in their "Ivory Towers"
For once in deep sleep what rules your dreams
Is it thoughts of what you are or might have been
Maybe it's the way your subconscious mind
Portrays you as a Princess or a Queen
Maybe you will dream of a flight high above in the sky
Perhaps laying on some Sun-kissed beach upon the sand
Or Gambling in the Casino with Lady Luck
Hoping she will deal you a winning hand
But long before you know the answer
From your slumbers you always quickly wake
And it's then that you make yourself a promise
That tonight you won't make the same mistake
So tonight when it comes to time to go to bed

Clear all of your worries from your mind
Then the bad dreams and nightmares will all disappear
Only sweet dreams and happiness will you find.

Dennis Shrubshall   29th January 2011

Belles and Beaux

With thoughts of love as you sit and wonder
In a world of loneliness
To listen to the words that you so want to hear
Or to feel the warmth of a sweet caress
As in the arms of a new found love
Encompassed by a warm embrace
Can this be the answer to a constant dream
Perhaps a beautiful future that you may face
That feeling of warmth as he enters the room
The fragrance of your new perfume
Where all your sadness ebbs away
There is happiness instead of gloom
A lovers tryst in the new born day
With a mind that is free from doubt
Memories of a darkened past
Ready to be cast out
So open your heart to a new found love
Peace and tranquillity without end
Hand in hand into the Sunset
Just a Belle and a Beau, her new friend

Dennis Shrubshall   4th January 2012

Clovelly

There's a lovely little village
On the north coast of Devon
That stands out in my memory
For it's quaint and it's historic
A never changing example
Still there for everyone to see
Old cottages and shops
In a setting of great beauty
Evidence of many a bygone era
Carefully managed as a Civic duty
As you stand 400 feet high on the hill top
And the Sea comes into view
Down an ancient cobbled causeway
That you'll soon be walking through
It's downwards ever downwards
O'er the steps and slopes you travel
Passing all the antiquated shops and buildings
And your puzzled thoughts un-ravel
In wonderment at the way this village
Has stood the tests of time
To transport goods and chattels
To this Devon heritage sublime
Where conventional vehicles are forbidden
And only sledges are used
Which mystifies many of the visitors
Leaving some of them confused
All done to preserve the cobbled slopes

That to the 16th Century date
The value of this part of Devon's history
Is difficult to estimate
There's a sleepy little harbour
Boats hustling to & fro'
Mostly powered my diesel engines
But still some the stalwarts row
Fishermen still ply their trade today
On the quay with their catch or mending the nets
Ever conscious of the visitors eyes
Or perils of the Sea without regrets
There are Cream Teas or Sea Food on offer
Or a Sandwich with a beer or two
In a perfectly placed Hotel on the Quayside
Attracting customers as they're passing through
Dickens, Kingsley and Turner
Just a few of the names from the past
All fell for the charm of Clovelley
Where the hands of time never seem to run fast
And when you have seen all the sights there
It's time to return to the real world once more
You're faced with a mountainous half mile climb
Which you'll find is no mean chore
In the past the only transport was by Donkey
Now pensioned off as things of the past
And you can now return by Landrover
Less tiring and twice as fast
But I'm sure that after your visit
You will often turn over in your mind
The places you've visited over the years
Tho' not many as quaint you will find
And as you leave the delights of this north Devon village
And the thoughts on your visit you've reviewed
Drive south just a little further into Cornwall
To the nice sandy beaches of Bude.,

Dennis Shrubshall   16th October 2010

First Poem

Words are free to everyone
To use as best they may
And if you feel like poetry
Give it a try one day
Take some words and write them down
Juggle them around for a little time
And soon before your very eyes
You'll have written your verse in rhyme
It really isn't hard you know
Once your mind is set
On making your own composition
And your inhibitions you forget
You think of a suitable subject
And what you would like to achieve
Then think of words to match your thoughts
It's easier than you believe
The only tools you need for the job
A knowledge of words or a dictionary
And start to write to your hearts content
Lines and phrases that you can vary
Then juggle again with what is on the page
Until what you see seems right
Then read and enjoy what you've just composed
Poetic licence is within your sight.

Dennis Shrubshall   15th July 2012

Horizon

I look through the viewer
And what can be seen
Peace and tranquility
In the countryside serene
Flow gently Sweet Afton
Or so the poem goes
As the river seen here
So gently flows
Like the path of life
Till it disappears
Into the distance over the years
But still in the foreground
The trees stand so strong
As tho' watching the water amble along
Amid the reeds there sits a man with a wish
Perhaps today he'll be catching some fish
Is it the past or the future I see
On the horizon waiting for me
The houses so welcome
Somewhere to rest
After walking the countryside
The place I love best
To stroll through the meadows
Hear the song of a bird
Perhaps glimpse some cattle
Or horses preferred
As onward I amble

To the sunset I find
At a backward glance
The scenic beauty left behind

Dennis Shrubshall   27th August 2008

Life's Rainbow

To sit and close your eyes as tho' in sleep
Perhaps to reflect on events now past
Thankfully the Happiness you keep
But the scene before you leaves you aghast
For life is like the colours of the Rainbow
Stark but sometimes serene
With Pastels there in tranquility
To calm the turbulence in between
First you may notice predominance of blue
Representing the sky above
Tinged by the Golden rays of the Sun
To envelope you in a world of love
Then the change may be Oh! so rapid
As Pastels to Vibrants quickly alter
Reflecting the tumult within your soul
Could this be the moment you falter
It could move from Lilac to Mauve and onwards
Giving warning of trouble ahead
Followed by Mauve and Purple and Violet
And maybe a menacing Red
But if I were an Artist
This knowledge I could impart
To put this image on Canvas
Creating a work of Art
The Blue of the sky and the Sun up above
You're in a boat with the wind and the spray
You'll weather the Storm on Life's Ocean

And chase all your demons away
The pain and the sadness and sorrow in Life
Are depicted by the Vibrant colours severe
Then the Green and Lemon and Blue Pastels
Embracing friends and loved ones holding you dear
Look forward to a colourful existence
Forget about the danger of Red
Take each and every day as it comes
For " He who dares wins" it is said.

Dennis Shrubshall   13th January 2010

Miners

Once again another tragedy
Among the men who search for coal
Silence in the hills and valleys
Except for the Church bell's toll
For the men of Wales who spend their lives
In the depth and darkness of the pit
Toiling 'neath the bowels of the earth
Living on experience and wit
Eking out a living
From the job they know so well
Danger never far away
As miners will readily tell
So now our hearts go out to the Families
For the men that they have lost
Yet another mining disaster
Exacting it's human cost
Tho perhaps some day in the future
The need for mining will cease
But for the lads who lost their lives this day
May they ever Rest in Peace.

Dennis Shrubshall   16th September 2011

Old Father Thames

When you look back in time to London
Resting gently on the Bank of the Thames
How long we relied on these well known waters
Like Flower blossoms depend on their stems
For the River was like a huge lifeline
To bring goods and trade from abroad
Or maybe just ship coal from Newcastle
A form of transport they could then afford
As an island we relied on imported commodities
And the Sea the only method of transportation
Bringing food and materials from far off lands
To feed and cater for an ever growing Nation
The Thames at that time was like a main artery
With a constant flow of Maritime vessels to the heart
Of the City at the head of an Empire
From which their precious cargoes their final journeys
would start
The banks of the river were thronging with life
At jetties and quays along the river's side
Eagerly awaiting the turn round of Vessels
With the rise and fall of the tide
For some of the largest freighters
Their holds with cargoes filled to the brim
Needed all the skill of the river Pilots
To safely guide these vessels in
There were cranes and derricks and stevedores
Eager   to unload the cargo that the ships bore

And then load these cargoes on to barges and trains
And road haulage lorries by the score
The bulk was carried overland by rail
On a network Oh! so vast
And many a tear was shed by the men of the River
When Sea transport became a thing of the past
The Docks were all closed and their warehouses
demolished
And a vast building site the area became
Producing up-market properties for the affluent society
From then the London riverside was never the same
But in the still of the evening if you're down by the river
And sit with your eyes closed I'm sure
You'll see the vast Armada of shipping that graced those
waters
And the barge steered by the skill of the lighterman's oar

Dennis Shrubshall   22nd March 2010

Speak to an Angel

So many thoughts go through your head
When you sit at rest and close your eyes
The Memories come flooding back
And it's then that you realise
The hands of time are ticking by
And life so quickly moves along
Then friends we know must leave this world
And we are left to mourn but yet keep strong
To follow in those well trodden footsteps
As we carry on our daily Lives
With an ever constant vision in mind
Making sure that the friendship thrives
Though they will not pass this way again
When their life on earth reached it's end
But you feel that you can't lose contact
With that relative or friend
So how do you speak to an Angel
As she flies along majestically over the cloud
Do you use your voice in a normal tone
Or maybe shout a message out loud
A message for a special someone
Who's with you in your thoughts each day
Or something for those dear friends in the past
To let them know that they're never far away
So what do feel are the things you want to say
What are the loving thoughts that come to mind
Or is it just enough to live the rest of your life

In those knowledgeable footsteps left behind.

Dennis Shrubshall   6th September 2011

The Royal Marine Medic

When young you may yearn to be a Military Man
And look forward to fulfil your dream
Your head is full of various choices
And some you may take to extreme
You could choose to join the Army as a Soldier
Or the RAF to be a pilot and fly
There's always the Navy who are looking for Sailors
With shore postings where you'll keep your feet dry
But the young man I have in mind made an instant
decision
A Royal Marine he decided to be
And after extensive courses of training
His dream became reality
His Uniform he donned with pride
The coveted Green Beret he was now able to wear
In the Service of his Queen and Country
And opted to a life of care
For he chose not to take a Combatant Role
And a Military Medic he became
Tho' he learnt how to use a Bayonet and Rifle
He acquired the necessary skill
Then he learned the art of a Medical Man
He opted to save life rather than kill
And after training he was posted to places far and wide
To any country in need of Military aid
To witness the horror and savagery of war
An also the Heroism so often displayed

For him Humanity is his ultimate Goal
Regardless of Colour or Culture or Creed
He is bound, as are Doctors, by the Hippocratic Oath
Where the preservation of Life applies to him indeed
Many times he will witness his colleagues under fire
Exploding IED's and a Snipers bullet passing his head
The smell of Cordite and the screams of Soldiers injured
Lost Limbs , bullet wounds and tending the dead
But he may also find he's faced with an injured enemy
soldier
Tho' it matters not he'll treat them just the same
Even put his life at risk to save an injured colleague ,
under fire
He sees it al as parft of the Medics game
And in battle sometimes civilians will suffer
 Horrific injuries and their lives are defiled
Althoug it's not unknown that he may be reduced to tears
As he battles the odds of time to save the Life of a child
The virtual weapon that he uses in his constant fight to
save lives
Some say must be in his healing hands
And the dedication to his Medics duty
Which unfortunately some people cannot understand
The life he leads is not for the money
But for the joy on a survivors face is his reward
To know that he has given them another chance at life
A luxury they thought they could never afford
And when his military days are over
His Civilian Life may very well depend
On whether the Trauma and the Heartbreak and the
Horror
Had brought his Military Career to an end
But fortunately that was not the case for this man
For he is now back home once more
Knowing ne'er again will he have to face the casualties
Away on some far flung Foreign Shore

Dennis Shrubshall   15th March 2011

Thoughts of Romance

Do you sometimes sit back and think of the time
When you and your soul mate first met
As you lived life to the full, enjoyed every minute
There was nothing for you to regret
Is that moment still clear when you both first held hands
And looked into each others eyes
Were your thoughts ever clear at the onset
Did you honestly visualise
That this was the start of a beautiful friendship
As on life's road you both now ambled along
Did you both meet each others expectations
Were there times when you thought you may be wrong
Do you remember well that first loving embrace
Face to face your lips met for the very first time
Did you close your eyes as tho' in a dream
Would this be your romance sublime
Then you walked together week after week
Eventually turning to months and then years
Were your lives filled with fun, love and laughter
Interspersed here and there with a few tears
Was your life like a Fairy Tale or Love Story
Where love perhaps rules your mind
Or was this just a happy natural union
Two lives romantically entwined
Did your Beaux bend and kneel when he asked for your hand
Was the courtship short or long after that first kiss

Was the Wedding grand, were you in Wonderland
Did it all end in wedded bliss
So now with a lifetime before you
You could walk to the Rainbow's end
Will you " be together until death you should part"
On the cards you're dealt by Fate that will depend.

Dennis Shrubshall   27th February 2011

A Winter Walk

It's early morning in December
A chill wind fills the air
As we stroll through the countryside
Without worry or care
For this is the Ramblers paradise
As we stroll along side by side
And a Rabbit dashes for cover
From the predators to hide
And there in the hedgerow
A wily Fox we espy
Vanishing into the undergrowth
Whilst we're passing by
The sun has not yet risen
As we were out with the dawn
The time for Nature lovers
To see the best of the morn
The frost in the treetops
Like a silvery gown
And as the birds flutter in the trees
Causing particles to drift down
On the unsuspecting travellers
Who are walking below
Sometimes the fall is heavy
Giving a semblance of snow
There are horses in the field now
And may have been there for days
Searching the frosty landscape

For some fresh grass where they may graze
Although it's early on Sunday
Some folk still have a daily chore
To round up the Dairy herd
For the Milking shed once more
Then onward we walk now
In the early morning mist
Never knowing what we might see next
To add to an ever-growing list
Of the wonders of Nature
On which people write and talk
And today we're the lucky one's to see them
On our Sunday morning Winter Walk

Dennis Shrubshall   2nd January 2011

Ultimate Dream

The ultimate dream for me as a lad
A Soldier I wanted to be
To follow the Family tradition
As part of the British Military
My Dad, Grandad & Uncles
All serving men were they
They did their time in uniform
Much like the lads of today
For some their Honoured Regiments
And their Heroes long since gone
Victims of amalgamation
But Family pride still carries on
So I signed on the line for 22years
A Lifetime man I wanted to be
To enjoy my life in a career of my choice
In the hope that the World at large would I see
The training was hard, but I coped with that well
As had all my relations before
For I knew that all the skills that I learnt
Maybe my lifeline in any Theatre of War
But since that time many postings I've had
On a War footing or keeping the Peace
But sometimes here in the United Kingdom
When those particular Hostilities were to cease
I've seen cruelty and horrors beyond imagination
But I've also witnessed Happiness and Joys
When you liberate a country from oppression

And see a smile on the face of the girls and boys
On the down side I've lost some best mates in battle
At times I admit I broke down and cried
As they returned home in a Union Flag covered coffin
But for me it released the deep emotion I stored inside
And now as I come to the end of my Service
22 years I've served the Country ,Flag and the Queen
In my head will I retain the scars of Service, for Life
Of the Death and Destruction I've many times seen
But I count myself among the lucky ones
For I have been to the gates of Hell and back
And if I was asked to do the same thing again
I know no enthusiasm would I lack
But I know when I walk through the closing Barrack Gates
At "Attenshun" I'll stand in Silent Tribute
To all my mates and colleagues that made the Ultimate
Sacrifice
And give them all just one long Final Salute.

Dennis Shrubshall   12th December 2009

The Simple Life

Whatever happened to the simple life
Where people were carefree and gay
Even the word at the end of the last line
You mustn't mention today
We live for political correctness
No inference should ever be used
As there might be misinterpretation
And cause persons to be confused
You've got to be very careful
With a colour scheme on your mind
'cos if black is one of your choices
Some opposition you might find
Be careful to add in some Yellow and white
When decorating a home that's palatial
And throw in some red & green & blue
Or someone might suggest that you're racial
Don't try to buy a Golliwog Doll
Or a Teddy bear try to name
As it might be misinterpreted in Arabic
And you'll be the one that takes the blame
You may walk in the street and be confronted
And feel on your handbag a tug
As you turn you may see a young hoodlum, in a "hoodie"
You're now the victim he's trying to mug
But you don't give in without fighting
With your fist you catch him full in the face

To the do-gooders you're now not the victim, but
assailant
And the Police cart you off in disgrace
With young thug getting compensation
And then disappear without trace
So now if you will cast your mind back
To the times when you were but a mere Child
And Angels we certainly were not
Standards of behaviour were stringent
And wrongdoings were never forgot
Perhaps the fear of the Policeman's gauntlet
Or a swipe round the head with his Cape
Or his threat to tell all to your Father
Then you knew there was no escape
Even the criminal fraternity knew
That if knife or a gun they should use
The Law then was very specific
And they would die in the Hangman's Noose
So now as I sit and contemplate
And slowly close my eyes
Whatever happened to the simple life
I'll leave you all to visualise.

Dennis Shrubshall   11th December 2007

The Peacock

The world has a wealth of beautiful birds
In colours and culture serene
Flying the skies or swimming on water
Always a joy to be seen
But the species I have in mind today
Natives of India are they so I'm told
Proud and pretty and colourful are Peafowl
A wondrous joy for the spectator to behold
There are varying species of Peacocks
With exotic colours and hue
Black Shouldered, Congo, Green and White
And of course there's the Indian Blue
These birds are known to need companionship
And the Peacock leads a very full life
For he may befriend a harem of 2 – 5 Peahens
Not satisfied with just one wife
Each bird has a multi feathered train
Which in fact will cover a brown tail
When mating the Peacock will spread it's train
Forming a huge and Kaleidoscopic fan
Containing every conceivable colour
Possibly known to man
He'll vibrate his tail at the Peahen
And all his prowess in awe he'll display
In a valiant effort to impress the female
And mate so that eggs she may lay
The eggs that she'll lay aren't much larger than a chicken

And after 28 days the chicks may hatch
But some females lay decoy eggs away from the nest
In order that their predators they despatch
The young chick will walk less than one day old
And when born, with flight feathers on their wings they're endowed
Then before the end of the first week they can fly
Making their mother the Peahen very proud
For in the wild they'd be subject to predators on the ground
Necessitating the need for them to fly
And find safety in the trees of the forests at night
In safety knowing Mother's very close by
The Peacock is a bird of great beauty
Especially as his male talent, his feathers he deploys
But you'll know every time there is imminent   danger
As he emits quite a loud recognisable noise

Dennis Shrubshall   16th July 2011

Seasons

Seasons are noticed in the countryside
Far more than a City or Town
As that is where one is nearest to Mother Nature
And is seen in the colour of her gown
In Winter she may wear a cloak of sheer White
With Silver tinges of Frost here and there
But this is the time when her Plants and Flowers may
suffer
When not treated with infinite care
And slowly we move on to the approaching Spring
As gradually the climate may change
With Crocus and Snowdrops and Jonquils and Daffodils
Some of Natures extensive Range
As they nudge their way though the chilly soil
To get warmth and a glimpse of the Sun
Quite a lot of the trees are starting to show their buds
As though the run-up to Summer has begun
The Regal Camelia had blooms which have now faded and
died
But her foliage remains shiny and proud
The trees that shelter the Flower beds from the wind
With a cloak of green are now richly endowed
And among them the stately Magnolia
Whose bloom life is short I must say
For as soon as they are showing in all of their glory
Gales force winds seem to blow them away
Then the first Roses open wide their pretty coloured heads

As tho' to announce Summer's now here, out loud.
With blooms of every imaginable colour
Enough to make any avid gardener proud
Even the grass is growing and changing
To a healthy shade of green
On the lawns that lay around the Flower beds
And the little paths in between
Mother Nature is now here in her glory
In a magnificent Gown of Gold
To match the endless hours of Sunlight
For the eye a wondrous sight to behold
The fruit on the trees are well formed now
As they ripen and become mature
Before the leaves that surround change from green to gold
To form an Autumnal scene demure
The life of the flowers has come to an end
They bow their heads and then seem ready to die
As the temperatures drop in the twilight
And the first hint of Frost is in the clearness of the sky
Dahlias and Fuchsias were in full bloom
Just a few days looking back
But suffer as victims to Winter's first Frost
Overnight they wither and their heads turn Black
For it's sad to witness this drastic change
That Mother Nature knows so well
As she draws a Winter Cloak around her
The Icy winds perhaps to repel
So it's time now to prune the plants and shrubs
Remove all dead foliage too
Perhaps plants next Season's Bulbs & Tubers in Tubs
So in the Spring their pretty heads will show through
The lawn has had it's last Autumn trim
And the Flower Beds are turned for the last time
Now is the time for Mother Nature's Children to sleep
Perchance to survive Winter's chilly clime
'Til once again with the advent of Spring
Along with the warm morning dew
There is evidence of new growth awakening
For Mother Nature's early Floral Review.

Dennis Shrubshall   6th October 2009

Oh! Woe is me

Oh! Woe is me what's happened
Where has my work all gone
Someone's pinched all my poems
Perhaps used them for their own
I thought that posted here
For other Members to read
Could be a way of sharing
Without their safety I would exceed
Maybe they've been removed to the archives
Or on the furnace been tossed
As they are freely posted
It couldn't have been the cost
But no doubt in the near future
The mystery may be solved
And hopefully the villain apprehended
For the crime in which he was involved
'tis fortunate tho' with a P C
Copies of all you keep
Laying on your hard-drive
In the hours that we sleep
But I'll keep a special vigil now
Less into my Office they creep
So now I've tried to find the Answer
From, Bob, who for knowledge is a glutton
Who after extensive thought decreed
Delete the names from your "ignore" button
So now the problem is solved

And all my doubts are put to bed
But if nothing else it gave me a reason
To write a rhyme instead .

Dennis Shrubshall   30th August 2009

"Muppet"

If you cast your mind back over the years
Perhaps as a child at school
When Mum would wait at the school gate
Nobody inside the gate was the rule
And as the parents met and chatted
Perhaps about shopping they had to get
Or all manner of everyday things
But sometimes to admire another Mum's pet
For this was the time the parents used
To give exercise to their pet
And often inspired other parents
A gift for their child they might get
So they'd broach the question quite nicely
And if a canine friend their children might please
They'd browse thro folders and brochures
To see if they'd select one from these
There were Corgi's, Red Setters and Poodles
Some Chihuahua's and German Shepherds too
Dachshunds, Beagles and Airedales
Dalmations, Shih Tzu's to name but a few
Pomeranians, Border Collies, Weimaraners
Rottweillers make some people sigh
Having looked at all these wonderful breeds
'T was the Jack Russell that caught their eye
When the cheeky young Puppy came before them
A feisty young fellow was he
As if saying go on then buy me please

And a very good Family pet I will be
So home he went them that very d ay
The children were really very glad
As he was very small they named him "Muppet"
He was the first pet they'd ever had
Jack Russell's are playful and mischievous too
In confinement their freedom they'll seek
So he was kept on a lead or well fenced enclosure
And no destruction or havoc did he wreak
But he did all the things that new puppies do
"wee'd" on the mat and ran away
But very quickly learned that wasn't the thing to do
But carry out that function whilst out to play
And as the weeks passed by more adventurous Muppet
became
Left on his own a slipper or a shoe he would chew
Then hide behind the settee a she knew he'd done wrong
And realised chastisement was due
When walking in the fields they had to take great care
As "Muppets" hunting instincts might draw him away
And it's not too unknown for dogs of his breed
To run down rabbit burrows and there stay
After a good outing and returning home again
He's run around with the children and play
And then quickly eat his food followed by a drink
And settle in his basket for the rest of the day
When the owners went to bed he slept in a wire enclosure
With ample room to move about I have to say
Waiting for the morning sound of someone in the kitchen
To be let out to start another day

Dennis Shrubshall   12th February 2012

Just a Little Dewdrop

I'm just a little Dew drop
Laying on the leaf
Of a beautiful Flower
With it's petals underneath
But now my peace is broken
Someone's cut the flowers for a Floral display
And me just a little dewdrop
Here on the lawn must lay
And soon will come the Sunrise
To warm another day
And as the temperature rises
I shall evaporate away.

Dennis Shrubshall   24th September 2011

Guardian Angel

She's sitting now upon a cloud
Floating aimlessly through the sky
Surveying the world from above you
With an ever watchful eye
And you know she's your special Angel
Even though you may sleep
For she is the one that watches over you
And her heavenly watch she'll keep
For everyone needs some comfort
Maybe not from high above
Perhaps embraced in thoughts of one held dear
With arms outstretched with love
But life is full of complexity
Evident over the years
Sometimes brimming with happiness
Some occasions gently tinged with tears
If it were set as an image by an artist
On a canvas and easel displayed
Using oils and acrylics on a brush
Universal tools of the trade
All set on a natural background
Pale blue depicts the sky
Delicate shades of white and grey
For the clouds that go gently drifting by
Then what goes on below them
The richness of Life in varying shades of green
And here and there the Anger and Envy

In Vibrant colours can be seen
So study the painting carefully and you'll see
In pale Lilac with Silver wings
Your very own Guardian Angel
And the comfort her presence brings
So when next time you fall asleep
Maybe perchance to dream
You're sure to sleep contented
With her reign Eterrnal and Supreme

Dennis Shrubshall   6th December 2011

The Falklands War

When we left the shores of England
Bound for some distant land
Few of us knew of the Falklands Isles
Far less the job in hand
But once again we were called to fight
And an Island of oppressors rout
Yet another outrageous invasion
By Argentinia , territorial laws to flout
But they had not realised the anger they caused
As the Falkland Islands they tried to steal
For it activated a British resolve
And soon retribution the Argentinians would feel
With the target so far from the British mainland
14 days sailing maybe
So serious was this threat they posed
That a huge Armada set to sea
But the Submarine branch of the Royal navy was first
To arrive upon the scene
Alerted to the Islands by and S O S signal
From men of the British Royal Marine
Who had discovered the plight of the Islanders
And Argentinian prisoners they soon became
Who waited the arrival of the British Task Force
To put these invaders to shame
HMS Conquerer had the General Belgrano in her sights
When the orders came to Destroy
Which took but 3 of her Torpedoes, carefully aimed

And then to other duties deploy
But the Royal Navy suffered attacks from the air
And the Sheffield among those to be hit
Along with the RFA Sir Galahad, a tragedy
Like a gigantic bonfire was lit
Then the injured and wounded were air-lifted off
For them it was the end of their fight
But only the start of the battle, for their colleagues
As they marched off into the night
The SAS were swiftly deployed
The Airstrip at Pebble Island was their aim
To disable it's use for the Argentinian Air Force
And allow the RAF to land just the same
In order to bring in much needed supplies
That were needed in order to sustain
A concerted Military effort
So that the Islands they may regain
Helicopters too could use that facility
To land supplies and evacuate injured too
Back to the Hospital ships awaiting offshore
They all had a task to do
Goose Green , Tumbledown & Mt William
All names that come readily to mind
To all of the British Army soldiers
Who yomped across the Falklands , the "Argies" to find
But once again as is always the case
Any conflict has a terrible cost
Young men who are permanently injured for life
And the hundreds of young lives that are lost
This particular theatre of war continued
In horrendous conditions which were extreme
And the lads did the job as they only know how
Work together each one part of the big team
The RAF, The Royal Navy and the Army
United , as one, in this strategic fight
To rid the Islands of oppressors
And put an end to the Islanders plight
So once again the Union Jack could fly high on the
Flagpole
As a signal of freedom once more
But sadly many soldiers never saw their achievement
For they were the victims of the Falklands War .

Dennis Shrubshall   14th June 2009

Oliver Cromwell

On an April day in 1599
Oliver Cromwell was born
In Huntingdon in Cambridgeshire
In a country always torn
With politics and religion
A part of daily life
His parents were of minor landed Gentry
Far removed from poverty and strife
A University education at Cambridge
With all the knowledge he learned
And when he graduated
To Politics his hand he turned
In 1628 his birthplace he represented
In the House of Parliament for just one year
And then went through a religious crisis
Should he be a servant of God for his career
As radical Puritan he began to make his name
In 16 40 he entered Parliament once more
Charles 1 and Parliament were in disagreement
Which then turned into Civil War
Cromwell lacked in Military experience
He created and led "Ironsides" respected Cavalry
In 1642 when it all started
He rose from Captain to Lt. General with victory
Convincing Parliament to form a Professional Army
And then into battle at Naseby they went
To break the Kin's alliance with the Scot's

And their defeat was subsequent
Now Cromwell had established himself
As a Leader in the public's eye
His actions brought about the trial of King Charles
Andin 1649 by execution he was to die
He sought to win support for a new Republic
Suppressing radical elements in his Army so new
Becoming Lord Lieutenant of Ireland
Crushing garrisons at Wexford and Drogheda too
In 1650 defeated supporters of Charles 11 at Dunbar
And in 1651 at Worcester too , then on to 1653
Effectively ending the Civil War
And further credit in his personal history
He then carried out the "Dissolution of the Rump"
Or "Barebones Parliament" which gave him renown
In 1657 at home he became the Lord Protector
After refusing the Offer of the Crown
He reorganised the Church, Puritanism he established
Readmitted Jewish people back into Britain once again
And presided over religious tolerance
In order the peace to maintain
He ended the war with Portugal and Holland
And allied with France against Spain
Defeating them at the Battle of Dunes
And then returning home once again
Although he returned once again a victor
Defeating once again the foreign foe
It was only months later that he met his demise
And in London he died but with nothing to show
And after the Restoration his body was exhumed
In retribution or so some said
To be hung and put on public display
Even though he was already dead
Richard Cromwell was named as his successor
As Lord Protector he reigned for 1 year
Unable to reconcile the various factions
He abdicated only to disappear
He fled to Paris for more than 20 years
And in 1680 back to England he came
Living here until his death
Under an assumed name

Dennis Shrubshall   11th December 2011

Army Life

When you sign on the line to be a Military man
After much thought and consideration
It is usually met by other Family Members
With a hint of worry and some trepidation
It is not a subject to be met lightly
When a Service career you wish to pursue
As it differs so much from Civilian life
Where discipline will be ultimate to you
No more can you adopt a carefree approach
As you travel through life the Army way
Where you'll be trained to act as a Team together
And your lives may depend on it one day
In the past the situation varied slightly
When Conscription was necessary to fill the need
Where Civilians under Mandate had to leave chosen
Professions
And were trained to fighting units at speed
But they all fought together in Combat
As loyal Brothers in Arms side by side
For in battle the enemy was never selective
And sadly both Conscripts and Regular soldiers died
But even today as in all those years ago
We have Territorials or "Terriers" for short
Always fully trained ,on standby, for emergencies
In case there were battles to be fought
So now you have made the decision
To follow in the Military path of those before

Where you'll carry out the role of a Professional Soldier
And operate in any chosen necessary Theatre of War
You'll don the Uniform of one of Britain's chosen
Regiments
To serve the Country, the Flag and the Queen
Act as Guard, Liberator or Peacekeeper
All this maybe for a lad just a mere Eighteen

Dennis Shrubshall   20th February 2010

A Mother's love is Eternal

The one thing I learnt very early in life
The importance of a Mum & Dad
The love of a Happy Family
Tho' riches we never had
And as I read the words you wrote
It all quickly came back to me
For the hands of time keep rushing by
But it is easy for me to see
That you are now faced with the sadness
Of the loss of a Mum so dear
Who cherished and fed and loved you all
And shared many a laugh and a tear
When young she clothed and fed you all
And bathed your wounds when you fell and bled
Comforted you all when you were worried
And tucked you up safely in bed
She knew the meals you loved to eat
And the clothes you were keen to wear
Encouraged you with your education & sport
All part of a loving Mother's care
With Dad as a partner to all of these chores
As a Family you work as a team
Living life for Happiness
Your success in life was your Mother's dream
She saw you through the rough and the smooth
Sometimes with an aching heart
But then like a bolt from the blue it happens

Sadness causes the tears to start
And as with us all the loss of a loved one
Leaves us empty and full of sorrow
But know they would want us to be strong
And face the world tomorrow
For no-one can remove those wonderful memories
Sacred to you and your Family tho' you sleep
As a Mother's love is eternal
And her Heavenly watch on you she'll evermore keep

Dennis Shrubshall   19th June 2010

A'Sailing we will go

We're tied alongside the dock now
Waiting for the tide to rise
And soon we'll be setting sail again
Under the clear blue skies
But there upon the Horizon
A hint of cloud in the sky
As we check the forecast for wind speed
And the sail lashings untie
It's time for us to leave now
And the mooring ropes we shed
Bound for another sea adventure
And wonder what lies ahead
The diesel engine's running smoothly
And down the estuary we move
Hoping for a change in the wind
Our sailing to improve
For now we are clear of the river
Out into the open sea
I wonder what today will bring
Perhaps something new to me
So it's time to unfurl the sails now
And watch as with wind they billow
And push our vessel across the waves
As a head laid gently on a pillow
For a sailor can liken a trip to a bed
Under the skies where he can live his dreams
Which sometimes turn to nightmares

In storms and rain that teems
We're sweeping over the waves now
Travelling at reasonable speed
And it's time to let out the Spinnaker
When all our hopes we'll exceed
To travel the English Channel and back
In the shortest possible time
Hoping for no serious difficulties
That means the Mast we'd have to climb
But with the Tide and a good wind behind us
We soon made the coast of France
But now we hope for a change of wind
That our return journey will enhance
For if the wind were behind us again
On the long journey back
It would cut the need of a sailors art
Without necessity to tack
As we glide along in silence
Bar the sound of the Sea on the bow
And the screech overhead of the Seagulls
We're in sight of the English Coast now
So it's time to reel in the Spinnaker
Perhaps enjoy a "tot" or two
As we're getting ready to enter the River again
When there's plenty of chores to do
We've stowed away the foresail now
As we approach the estuary quite fast
With only the mainsail catching the wind
As our journey is nearly past
So once again we hear the gentle throb
As the diesel motor we start again
To aid us into a docking position
And a manageable speed maintain
Then lower the remaining sheet from the wind
At the dockside we moor up Bow and Stern
And I wonder how many more trips like this,it takes
Before Sailsmanship I'll eventually learn

Dennis Shrubshall   28th June 2009

Bygone days

Memories are something we closely guard
As images within the mind
A constant record of times that have passed
For life has left them behind
But ever there for instant recollection
Whenever there is need
To illustrate how your life was, in an instant
Or personal knowledge may have been decreed
And for me I often sit and turn back the clock
To a time I remember when I was only three
For my Parents were only ordinary working folk
And never luxuries did they ever see
The lights in our cottage were powered by Gas
Mum cooked on a Kitchener Stove too
And a sink in the Scullery with cold water only
And there was still all the clothes washing to do
Next to the back door was the Wash-house
With a large Washtub encased in brick
And beneath it was a space for tinder and coal
In order to heat the required water fairly quick
Laundry was scrubbed on a rubbing board
To get out the ingrained dirt or grime
Then it was all placed in the Wash-tub
And through the old Cast Iron Mangle when it was time
Fridays was bath night just once a week
In a galvanised bath in front of the fire
Water was heated in the Wash-tub in the Wash-house

And then in buckets to the bath to forfill your weekly desire
My Sister was the only Girl you see
So she had the pleasure of the first bath every week
Then it was the turn of me and four brothers
Who had the water that was left so to speak
My Dad only earned 35 shillings a week
And out of that 4shillings and ninepence was rent
Yet somehow they managed to rear a Family of six children
With the rest of his wages carefully spent
The food that we ate was plain and inexpensive
And we were always well fed and warm
With love always there, in abundance, from our Parents
To make sure that we came to no harm
New clothes didn't come very often, but we knew
That a visit to the Co-op would be made
To acquire the necessary clothing or shoes
Then 2 shilling weekly instalments would be paid
So how would you compare those times to nowadays
Where affluence rules it would seem
But so many people in the world today
Expect to live life with luxuries extreme
But do all these things add up to the happiness
That I experienced when I was a mere child
This is something on which you must ponder
Or let your imagination run wild.

Dennis Shrubshall   11th February 2010

Despair

When you sit alone in the Eventide
And review the day that has passed
Do you ever give thought to those less fortunate
For if you did you may sit there aghast
Just imagine spending your life alone
As well as in the depths of despair
For them there is no one to turn to for guidance
Not a solitary person to care
As they spend their days in what could be a Prison cell
But for Prisoners visitors are allowed
For these unfortunate people
They are alone even though in a crowd
It is hard to understand what goes through their mind
So if you asked them they probably couldn't tell
Of the problems and worries that surround them
Even though they look healthy and well
Can you think what it's like not to see another soul all day
With nobody to turn to for advice
Cocooned in a lifetime of solitude
Where outsiders live their lives so concise
So stop if you will and consider, long and hard
Can you think of some such person who needs some care
Maybe then with arms open wide you can embrace them
And guide them from their solitude and despair.

Dennis Shrubshall   11th October 2009

Hope and Faith in times of need

The path of life is a winding trail
Help always seems out of sight
Especially when you are alone with your thoughts
In the early morning or late at night
You try to find the answer
To the many problems on hand
But someone , somewhere holds the key
And tries to understand
The traumas which beset you
In your bid to do what is right
To agree to Mum's operation
And perhaps put an end to her plight
But the thing to always remember
As you peer out into the gloom
It won't be long before Mum's on her feet
Perhaps with a frame
To help her across the room
For she needs the strength
Which I know you conserve
To deal with your dear Mother's health
It takes tolerance and consideration
And Love and devotion
And I know that it's there in great wealth
As I write these words to you my friend
I hope guidance and comfort they give
As everyone needs love and companionship
To make this world a fine place to live

Dennis Shrubshall   30th March 2009

Lost in an Alien world

I close my eyes and try to think
Of a world I may have left behind
Thoughts go flashing through my head
Am I really losing my mind
I seem to be in an alien world
Bereft of the life I knew
Full of nightmare images
Can the things I see be true
Why has my world turned around so
For I've caused nobody harm
And as I survey my surroundings
All I see is hatred and alarm
Where can I turn to for safety
Is there shelter away from this tempestuous storm
Maybe someone to embrace me
And keep me free from all harm
How I long for the life I knew
It seems Oh! so long ago
When I was treated like a Princess
As I lay in the arms of my Beau
And he lovingly gently caressed me
He knew all the right things to say
So far away from my world of today
Hostility reigns everywhere
Am I really one of life's cast off's
Surely someone must care
And help me to lift this shroud from my life

And take me back from Despair
Then whilst these thoughts were in my head
A curtain appeared to rise
A reassurance came from within my soul
That now I must open my eyes
And lo and behold there before me
The Sun was Gold and the Sky was Blue
A welcome back to a carefree world
The gates open to pastures new
Once more love could be within my grasp
No more would I need to hide
Throw open my arms and embrace the world
Perhaps with a new loved one by my side

Dennis Shrubshall   15th December 2010

Newly Wed

As a Bride she was a pretty girl
Oh! such a lovely sight
With Wedding Dress and train as well
Her body festooned in White
But when it came to time for bed
In "nightie" and long white drawers
Because she knew it only too well
Her Bridegroom perpetually snores
So in order to survive the Honeymoon
Without this couple coming to blows
She decided to end it there and then
And placed a peg on the end of his nose
Which cured the problem right away
For this newly wedded girlie
But in order to allay suspicion
The next morning she had to get up early
Remove the peg, and look serene
So when Hubby woke she would be seen
As a caring Wife with biscuits and cup of Tea
Matrimonial bliss
Assured of course that well she might
 Have to do the same again
Each and every night
Fancy doing that each day
Without shedding just a few tears
For all the rest of her married life
Perhaps another fifty years

Dennis Shrubshall   1st August 2008

Oh! To be in Essex now that Autumn's here

As one travels the lanes and byways
Of a rural community
The changing signs of the Seasons
Are very plain to see
You've seen Spring come and go
With Tulips and Daffodils galore
With Regal Camelias and colourful Magnolias
As Summer comes to the fore
Trees are in blossom and Roses too
Warmth of Sun fills the air
Encouraging plant- life to fruition
Flowers in beauty everywhere
But all too soon the Summer is fading
You'll notice the morning dew
As you walk through fields and foliage
Showing the spiders webs clearly too
The flowers all now seem to bow theirs heads
As once more their life comes to and end
And in gardens secateurs are now busy "dead heading"
To be used as compost " The GardenersFriend"
But back to our countryside ramble
Where the trees their leaves have changed
Leaves of Green and Gold and Russett
To form a carpet on the ground neatly arranged
It would appear that Mother Nature works in this way

As her matronly watch on the countryside she'll keep
Like a blanket to cover the plant life
During their long Winter sleep
So as your countryside ramble is nearing it's end
At this interesting Season of the year
The words that may be passing through your head
Oh! to be in Essex now that Autumn is here.

Dennis Shrubshall   1st October 2011

Poetic Licence

Hi Colleagues it's nice to read your words
That you write from time to time
And even more especially
Because you write in rhyme
It really is a pity
That others we can't enthuse
To join the thread in unison
Should they ever feel the muse
To sit and write some words of verse
For others to enjoy
For it matters not the subject
Or the method they employ
Should they see a passing Elephant
Or a hopping Kangaroo
Or even a local Aborigine
Playing his didgeridoo
Is that a Eucalyptus tree
And a friendly Koala Bear
'Cos they're all likely subjects
You can mention if you care
For they're things you see in Aussie
But if you're here in he U.K
You could write of the rain or the floods perhaps
Or yesterday's Sunny day
Then there's cattle and sheep
And people asleep watching a game of Cricket
Or kids in the park playing football

To see just how far they can kick it
You can ramble on for hours
But I think it is now the time
To write the last conclusive words
And bring to an end this rhyme

Dennis Shrubshall   7th August 2007

Response to Depression

Try if you will to close your eyes
And think of memories past
The times when you had a smile on your face
As on happiness your eyes you cast
But then your life has gone through change
Over these many years
With strain and stress and tragedy
Accompanied by tears
But this is the way that you relieve
The pent up feelings inside
Reality you can't run away from
For there is no place to hide
But if you look to the future
At the end of the tunnel there is light
And the end of your depressive state
As everything turns out right
With the help of the friends you know
Who will help you along the way
If not in fact in deeds themselves
They know the right things to say
To guide you back to the bright side of life
With understanding and tolerance shown
These are the things that prove to you
You will never be on your own
And then you will go from strength to strength
And search and find fields anew
In fact the world is your Oyster

And it's waiting just for you

Dennis Shrubshall   27th August 2008

Thanksgiving

This story started long ago
Across those miles of Sea
In the land we know as America
A far off land to me
The Pilgrim Fathers left their native land
Bound for foreign shores
Searching for a different life
Amongst the native Indians
To learn their traditions and their laws
Eventually landing at Plymouth
Or Massachusetts as it is now known
Strangers in a foreign land
Where the seeds of their new life would be sown
The early days were a struggle
For the 102 pilgrims that settled there
As lack of food was always a problem
But overcame by care
The Wampanoag Indians saw their plight
Providing seeds for them to cultivate
And even taught them how to fish
Supplying extra meals on their plate
They tilled the land and sewed the seeds
In 1621 their Harvest bore a good yield
And 2 years later with Governor Bradford
Thanksgiving day was revealed
Initially a "fast" and "feast" to celebrate
Successful harvest of crops from the ground

Becoming a long and lasting tradition
Celebrated through the years
By Americans right across the land
With lots of laughter and tears
Some say there is doubt where the day first started
Be it Virginia or Plymouth it seems
And even the dates tend to vary
If taken to great extremes
Abraham Lincoln during his term
In an effort to get North and South to unite
Proclaimed the date as Last Thursday in November
To last the whole day and night
It stayed that way until 1941in December
When Franklin D. Roosevelt made his decree
That the fourth Thursday in November , by Federal legislation
Was the day Thanksgiving would forever be
But in Canada it was slightly different
Because of the climate change
Their harvest were obviously earlier
So a more suitable date they had to arrange
In 1957 The Parliament of Canada had to decide
Once again their choice to decree
That the second Monday in October
Was when their Thanksgiving would be
So eat and drink and enjoy yourselves
What more is there for me to say
Be you Canadians or Americans
It's your Thanksgiving Day

Dennis Shrubshall   27th November 2011

The Major

Life is a story waiting to happen
As page by page it yields
A perfect image of any subject
Which covers so many different fields
But this is the tale of a young lad
Who dreamed as teenagers may
What was his ultimate goal in life
Which Career would he choose at the end of the day
Be a Surgeon , a Doctor or Deliver the mail
Learn to be a pilot or drive a train
The decision I'll try to explain
But his mind he made up and the option he chose
As already an Army Cadet was he
That he would be become a Soldier
And spend his life with the Military
As a raw recruit he found the going hard
But his ambition was always to succeed
So he settled into his Army Career
And sailed through his training with speed
Then it was time to become a Tradesman
And he covered that very well indeed
With the choice of Infantry, Signals or Artillery or
Transport
Perhaps he may have chosen Tanks
And with achievement ever present in his mind
Rose successfully through the Ranks
For here was a man who wore his uniform with pride

In the Service of the Country, The Flag and the Queen
Ever aware of the welfare of his colleagues
Making sure they all worked as a team
For when you are part of a Military Unit
Whether the role is to attack or defend
Discipline and dedication is of paramount importance
On which everyone's life may depend
His Hobbies included Ski-ing and Golfing
And loved friendships with Ladies too
An Artist with a talent for sketching scenes and people
A wealth of activities for him to do
But back once more to the Military man
Who with hard work quick promotion came his way
He rose to the rank of Major, with a motto
" Carpe Diem" which for him meant " Seize the day"
Standing tall and proud in his Uniform
Sporting Medals upon his chest
With "silvery" hair and a cheeky smile
The Army life is what suited him best
He's served in many parts of the World
And the horrors of various theatres of War
Also witnessed the smiles and admiration of the victims
Enjoying the Peace he'd been fighting for
Peacekeeping is never an easy task
None of these things are attained without cost
And the Major knows this only too well
Through the friends and colleagues he's lost
And now as this story is coming to a conclusion
The relevant points I've been asked to disclose
About a proud and compassionate Soldier
From a cadet to Major he rose
As he marches along with a Military stride
His task the less fortunate to defend
I for one would be pleased to shake his hand
As I bring his story to an end.

Dennis Shrubshall   24th April 2011

The Tramp

The Tramp as we know him
Here in the U K
Or maybe known as a Hobo
In the U S of A
His clothes are scruffy
His hair is unkempt
Everybody shuns him
Does it mean he's exempt
From the hand of kindness
Offered without malice
To a "man of the road"
Without a winners chalice
Wanders the roads and the ground is his bed
His belongings in a bag
Where he rests his head
Just someone who maybe down on his luck
On a meagre pittance trying to exist
When issuing the milk of human kindness
His were the hands they missed
So perhaps we should think hard
When next a Tramp you may meet
And remember these words which I often repeat
In a situation of any similarity
There but for the grace of God goes me

Dennis Shrubshall   11th April 2012

Times of change

I've been known to write an ode or two
Especially late at night
When I know folks might look for something to read
Or on a subject throw some light
For when you visit a Website
It opens your eyes to a different world
How other people lead their lives
Or sit in their armchairs neatly curled
Some like to join in an Internet quiz
Whilst others in a Forum debate
Arguing the pro's and con's of politics
Continuing online until quite late
Some may just enjoy a quiet read on their own
A short story or perhaps and odd ode
Written about a particular subject
Or maybe experience picked up on Life's road
And to some it seems strange how folks can just sit
And stare for hours at a computer screen
Conversing in text across the whole World
To persons they've not known nor even seen
But this has evolved in the World of today
Through technology at it's widest acclaim
The distance can be covered on the keyboard
Let your fingers do the walking is the name of the game
So close your eyes if you will now
And cast your mind back to the years that have flown
You can now sit alone in a room at your home

With a time machine of your very own

Dennis Shrubshall   29th September 2010

Take the Strain.

As you sit and ponder the rights & wrongs
As well as the maybe's too
Those thoughts that lie there in your head
Of the way that Life has treated you
It's never easy to understand
What fate may have in store
Especially when troubles abound
And then you find some more
Examples of thoughtlessness around you
Which inevitably cause pain
Even though un-intentional, perhaps
It creates an added extra strain
To endeavour to keep Life on an even keel
To deal with the matters in hand
And cope with all the pitfalls and trauma
And finish with everything well planned
For it is always hard to know someone you trust
Has not lived up to that esteem
But there is ever hope in your heart
Tho' distant it may seem
But to someone so resilient
With a spirit in your soul
You can fight the Devil and win , I know
So that once more your Life may be whole
And fill once again with the joy that you knew
Not very long ago
So throw open wide the windows of Life

And once more let the Happiness in
For with hope and faith and determination
Another battle you can win

Dennis Shrubshall   10th April 2009

Writing Today

Poems and Odes are more popular today
Than ever they've been in the past
'cos with your friendly computer for company
You can write down your thoughts really fast
Not like the days on the paper you'd scrawl
With a handy pencil or pen
And then get out your Erasor
And start all over again
It's easier to write and edit, if you must
There is much more time to think
Of a stimulating subject
That will take you to the brink
Of that vast vocabulary of words
Ever constant on your mind
Eager to spill out on to the screen
When a suitable subject you find
And you don't have to come to a conclusion
But "save as" till the next time you right
Whether today or tomorrow
Or even next Saturday night
Where in the interim period
The subject in your mind you will muse
On how your poem you will finish
What final line will you use
For the Start and Finale are important
Whether you joke or taunt ,sometimes tease
The ultimate aim of a writer

To hope their compositions will please
Those who find reading a pleasure
Scanning Poems and Odes in rhyme
And if a line or a verse brings a smile to a face
It's worth writing perhaps one more time .

Dennis Shrubshall   21st June 2008

A Midnight Swim

Day is ending night appears
As the end of the day I reach
Thoughts of a midnight swim perhaps
On some secluded beach
Stripped of all my clothing
Feeling the sand beneath my feet
Barely cool enough to walk on
After Summer's searing heat
The gentle waves lap along the shore
As into the water I stroll
Easing away the strain of the heat of the day
Which daily takes it's toll
Up to my waist and into the water
Swimming gently now
Head is clearing of worries
No frowns upon my brow
Arms and legs in unison
Water softly passing by
Heaven is here where I'm happy
In the Sea 'neath a moonlit sky
But sadly for me it seldom happens
It's merely a dream in my head
For I'm not an Oceanside dweller
But live and work in the City instead

Dennis Shrubshall   28th June 2012

The Old Shop

I take a walk to yesteryear
To see what I can find
What resourceful relic of the past
Has someone left behind
While walking down the country lane
There in front of me
Is this old fashioned brick building
Waiting for me to see
What treasures might I soon find
Forgotten memories unearth
Perhaps some National Heritage
Beyond monetary worth
The ancient ledge and braced stable-door
Fallen into dis-repair
And I walked beneath the arched head frame
To see what was hidden there
Various signs adorned the walls
Now with rust and dirt on top
Indicative that this quaint building
May have housed the Village shop
Where villagers may have purchased
Venus Soap or a pair of Frisby's Boots
For there were no Supermarkets then
Only this shop with local recruits
To man the tills and fill the shelves
And cater for what customers require
As they wander round selecting goods

Or just warm by the open fire
On the shelves there were glass stoppered jars
With sweets and biscuits inside
And a tug of the hand from the children
Expectant with eyes open wide
Or did Mum want some disinfectant
A loaf of bread and some butter and cheese
Perhaps some sausages, potatoes and carrots
To make a meal for her husband to please
All of this I imagined with my eyes closed tight
After a glimpse of the surroundings there
Standing in the remnants of a bygone age
Of a time when folks used to care
Where respect and reverence were an everyday occurrence
Sadly missing in my mind I must say
As I stepped once more into the daylight
After my trip to a long gone yesterday.

Dennis Shrubshall   28th September 2008

The Spiritualist

Religion gives grounds for many thoughts
As on life's road we stride
Ever keen to follow a faith
Perhaps cast all others aside
Muslims Jews and Christians
All have a place on this earth
But then there are many other sects
Each has a valued worth
Some people will pray to Allah
Many will worship at a shrine
Others put their faith in a Totem Pole
Each has a place and that's fine
I've read a little about Spiritualism
And that knowledge I'm here to relate
Facts that I have acquired
Though not able to substantiate
Curiosity started long ago, with
"Spirit Droppings" a publication for all to see
And read by all and sundry
But that was all so long ago in 1853
Heralding the belief in the spirit
That lives in the after world
Fosters belief in a new religion
The flag of Spiritualism unfurled
Where followers believe in the spirits
Of those who have gone before
Can be contacted by the living world

Maybe for evermore
In the early 1900's
Their membership had substantially grown
Their followers ever keen to learn
Of a Spirit World unknown
Contact was portrayed at a séance
Which Members could attend
Conducted by a Spirit medium
Who would try to contact a relative or friend
Whose spirit still lived after them
When they had left this mortal earth
Though sometimes remembered in prayer
With memories of great worth
They featured with the Abolition of Slavery
And the Suffragettes and their plight
A new and rising religion
Their new membership they might excite
Beliefs are strong as is their following
Both her and far away
For Spiritualist Churches there are many
Both in th U K and the U S A

Dennis Shrubshall   26th December 2011

When you come home again to Wales

To look across the hillside
As far as the eyes can see
Only the Mountains and Valleys
In sheer tranquility
Some of the peaks with snow atop
Seen from the valleys below
This is where scenic beauty lies
As all the tourists know
For Wales has long been noted
As the Land of Music and Song
Where you can go to sleep
Just counting real Sheep
Seen in the countryside all day long
For far away a voice is calling
Peels of memory chime
Come home again come home again
It said through the echoes of time
To welcome home Welsh patriots
To the mining villages past
And look if you will at the buildings
Still covered in a film of coal dust
To explore some of the Welsh history
But to gloss over would be unjust
Picture the scene in the early morn
As the Colliers walk through the village for their shift

There's even a hint of a song in the air
As their laden spirits they try to lift
And take those last few steps to the pithead
Can you imagine how they might feel
Gathered together once more in the hoist
As the tired cogs start to squeal
And lower these heroes to the bowels of the earth
Not knowing what they might find
To hack and pick and shovel coal
Leaving their wives and families behind
While they work in the damp and the darkness
Even ponies were blinkered there
And each one loved by the pitmen
They treated their favourites with care
It's hard to imagine the life that they lived
Below ground for all those hours
Hoping each day that aloft they'd return
To the welcome daylight and showers
But day after day , year on year
All some managed to achieve
Was to earn just a miserly pittance
And find it an effort to breathe
As older they grew but wouldn't give in
For they knew mining was in their blood
Their very existence relied on coal
Which they clearly understood
But sadly today the winches no long turn
To raise and lower the cage
As Coal Mining recedes into History
As a relic of a bygone age
And we go forward to a modern era
That Health & Safety would not condone
The un-healthly working environment
That Welsh Miners had always known
For many a Family the wrench was hard
Without Coal they had to adjust
And try to find other employment
To put food on the table, a must
I'm not too sure, for a Celt I am not
So it would have to be a pure guess
Not having to go down the pit again
Might have been worth just a little bit less
As long as body and soul were kept intact

For wives no longer necessary
To fear the sound of the siren, for an accident
Would it be their loved one,s they'd bury
I trust as this story is read now and then
Like other old Welsh tales
You remember the words of that famous song
"When you come home again to Wales.

Dennis Shrubshall   8th August 2008

Tiny Tots

Knit one Purl one Plain one
Is how the pattern goes
Knitting Squares and sewing them together
That's how the blanket grows
To cover up those tiny tots
Making sure that they'll be warm
Giving them some comfort too
Making sure they suffer no harm
For life so young is precious
Exacting extra care
Making sure in the early days
There's always someone there
To comfort them and feed them
And permanent watch to keep
Making sure of their safety
Even when they sleep
And after those worrying weeks have passed
Constant care enhanced each young child
Ensuring them of better life
And parents who are beguiled

Dennis Shrubshall   4th January 2012

Back in control

It takes a great deal of courage
To put down your thoughts in rhyme
To try to explain to others
How you may feel from time to time
Your past keeps returning to haunt you
Living deep within your soul
But now you're fighting those demons
And starting to have control
You've taken the step to share with others
What causes you to want to scream
A recurring constant nightmare
Instead of sleep perchance to dream
Tho pills may help to dull the pain
The memories don't seem to fade
But soon you'll notice the difference
With the courage you've displayed
For now you may travel the road ahead
Yours troubles will seem to fly
Along with the constant fear you've suffered
And thoughts you'd be better to die
For now there is light in the road ahead
A chance of return to your former self
And leave the terror and torment of the past
Well and truly packed on the shelf
To enjoy once again the life you enjoyed
With your loving family and friends
To erase those distant memories that returned

Each day as the night time descends
Peace & Happiness & Tranquility
Once again as you return from your life of hell
The gates of imprisonment swing open
Releasing you from your prison cell
So now you can move ever forward
You've conquered those demons within your soul
As a Soldier you've won the hardest battle of your Life
And you are the one in control

Dennis Shrubshall   9th December 2010

Raw Recruit

You've joined the Army to be a Soldier
That's all you ever wanted to be
To learn to be a Professional man
Away from your Family
And now as you walk through the barrack gates
Do you think your decision was right
'cos now you're part of the Military world
And not a civilian in sight
So it's off to your bunk in the billet
Which will be your home from now on
Away from all those home comforts
Which are now well and truly gone
Up for Reveille at 6 in the morning
And the Corporal is standing there
Right you lot, off down to breakfast
And then some drilling on the Square
Down to the Stores for Uniform issue
And then on to the M O for a check
To make sure that you're living and breathing
And the Sergeant lays his cards on the deck
"Now listen up and understand
And doubt me, well you might
'cos if you think my orders are wrong
These 3 Stripes on my arm make me right"
You'll do all your Basic Training
Will the shouting and bawling e'er stop
As you learn to obey the order of command

And at " double time" until you're fit to drop
Then on you go to learn a Trade
Perhaps to follow your Life's desire
To drive a lorry , a Tank ,Technical support
Or mend a puncture in a Transporter tyre
And when the training's all over
And you sit back and reflect
I wonder what your Life in the Army will bring
Perhaps more surprises than you expect
For the life of a Soldier is varied
There is always a call on his time
As the esteem of the British Military Man
Is held Worldwide as truly sublime
The task you face may be Overseas
To an unknown land afar
To help to solve a Terrorist threat
Or contain a local "Coups d'etat"
But whenever the World at large may need
The help of Military might
That is the time you've waited for
To use your training and join in the fight
Perhaps free other Nations of oppression
With the Pride that is always displayed
Which is always there in your Memory
Of your own "Passing Out Parade"
Now you've followed your Life's ambition
As a British Soldier to be seen
To wear your Uniform with pride
In Service of the Flag, the Country and The Queen .

Dennis Shrubshall   13th April 2009

Pitter Patter

As I turned my head from a Sun kissed Sky
Would the weather today stay this way
Or is the Barometer falling
Will we have rain back once more today
I glanced again across the room
As the Silver clouds go scudding by
Acting like a shutter to the Golden rays
The blue has disappeared from the Sky
And looking at the window
Droplets of rain a pattern they form
Is this a passing shower
Or start of a Summer storm
And a pitter patter melody plays
Beating upon the window pane
It might be even prudent to call it
The Rhythm of the Falling rain
But then as tho' by magic
It went as quick as it came
Leaving a Rainbow in it's wake
Is there a crock of Gold to claim
Now I'll cease my watch on the window
Until another day's here
When I'll look at the weather forecast
And check if the Barometer reads clear.

Dennis Shrubshall   16th October 2008

Life's Ocean

How long is a lifetime
I wonder every day
Where minutes seem to be like hours
As time drags on it's way
Where once I had the Midas touch
My dreams just turn to rust
All the things that I hold dear
Now crumble in my hands falling in the dust
How can my life have changed so much
Precious Memories seemingly lost
As I sail upon Life's Ocean
In stormy Seas I'm tossed
Sometimes when I'm tired and weary
And sitting all alone
I close my eyes and think of many things
In a Fantasy World of my own
The pent up emotions inside me
From the outside world I must hide
Yet never finding the answer I need
No matter how hard I've tried
All of these things going round in my head
As though in a perpetual whirl
Is this what happens to everyone
Or am I just an unfortunate girl
Then as I look through the window of my soul
A glimpse of Sunlight shines through the cloud
Happiness may be coming back to my life
Removing this eternal shroud

Dennis Shrubshall   5th May 2012

113

Golden days!!!

On Saturdays, Oh! so many many years ago
With no particular thought in mind
I went to the local dances with my Mates
To enjoy ourselves we were resigned
We sometimes went to the Ilford Town Hall
And would see the same girls week after week
But a change of tactics to Ilford Baths
Perhaps some new dance partners we'd seek
And in the Interval it was over to the local Pub
And if you'd played your cards right
Those Ladies would accompany you for a drink
And maybe let you take them home that night
Now the time that I speak of was a long time ago
In fact it was 1957, I think
When I met Doris Marjorie Rogers
She may have worn Red, Blue or Pink
To some it remained a mystery, for sure
'cos all of her friends called her Terry
Although Doris, her name, to her Family
To the others it was dance, drink and be merry
So onwards we go with the story
Before a few tears are shed
To the quaint Church on the Hill down at Pitsea
Where Terry and Dennis were Wed
On a freezing day in mid November
The Bride resplendent in white
For the Photos Den had to remove his Fairisle pullover

And nearly died of Frostbite
And then it was down to the little Church Hall
For a meal, some wine and a dance
Where the Family and friends would mix and chat
About how the Happy Couple met by chance
So onward they go to a little room at Ilford
To give married life a good try
And they worked hard and saved their wages
For the Bungalow that they would eventually buy
In 1959 and the Marriage going fine
Their first child Carole Anne was born
Which prompted their move to Benfleet
And their links with the City were torn
At a tender 3 month's old, with her parents
To the Bungalow , and give country life a try
With a lot of hard work before them
And an occasional tear in the eye
And after 2 more years
Of fun, laughter and the tears
The bright eyed Wendy Janice appeared 'pon the scene
To a Mum & Dad that's proud
To see that they've been allowed
An extension of the Family serene
But the children grew and married
And had families of their own
To Carole were Trudy, Jenny and Jassy
Three young ladies , my how they've grown
To Wendy the arrival of Matthew and Craig
Extended the family once more
And now Terry & Dennis have grandchildren 5
Where previously there were only 4
The very latest addition in kin
Isabelle is her name
Our very first Great Granddaughter
Six weeks ago into this world she came
As we come to the end of this story
That I'm reading to you here tonight
Do you think Terry married me for my money or good
looks
Or the lovely Poems that I write

Dennis Shrubshall   16th **November 2007**

Friends of Yesteryear

What happened to the friends of yesteryear
Where are they all today
How have they drifted away from your life
It's always hard to say
For when you are young you don't realise
Companionships happen quite fast
But friendships seem to take much longer
And they are the ones that may last
Remember for instance that last year at school
Where everyone had a best mate
But knowing how long it would stay that way
Was difficult to contemplate
Then on to a working environment
How did you cope with the vast change
Where now a lifetime's career you'd select
From a really enormous range
Did you make a new pal in those early years
Which into a fond friendship grew
Confiding in each others secrets
As you travelled these Avenues anew
But then the years flew by at incredible speed
And from teenage to adulthood you sped
Perhaps met your Belles or favourite Beaux
And finished up happily wed
But all the time this was going on
New lasting friendships were often made
Building a lifelong Amity

Over many a past decade
But as you grow older the list of friends of the past
Seems to diminish slowly year on year
And then the question comes to your mind
Will they all eventually just disappear
But you know in your heart that won't be the case
Some friendships are Eternal, never fear
So once again I'll pose this difficult question
What happened to all those Friends of Yesteryear

Dennis Shrubshall   16thOctober 2011

Daybreak

On the horizon the dawn is breaking
The air is wet with morning dew
Birds their morning chorus making
In the sky a hint of blue
Suddenly the Sun appears
Clouds are tinged with gold
Now the world is slowly waking
A glorious daybreak to behold
Is it April or September
Leaves of green or gold will tell
Calendar's not necessary
Signs of nature show me well
Mushrooms sprouting, there's some clover
Down the lane the tractor's roar
Once again the night is over
A country morn is here once more
Villagers now they are appearing
Noisy vehicles the silence take
But I alone am the lucky one
To witness a tranquil DAYBREAK

Dennis Shrubshall   *September 1994*

Caterpillar and Dewdrop

It's strange how rhyme can prompt replies
And the various responses made
Some are complimentary
Others are rather staid
But if I were a lonely Caterpillar
Surviving in a drought
I'd never survive on a Dewdrop
Of that there is little doubt
So in future I'll stay by the Lily pond
Where moisture is plentiful there
And leave the little Dewdrop
To evaporate in the morning air.

Dennis Shrubshall   October 2011

A Service Mum.

A woman's role is not an easy one
For she has many problems in life
Least of all the drastic change
From a single girl to a wife
She is no longer self reliant
But with Husband her services share
For that is what marriage is all about
Living life as a pair
But then there comes that patter of tiny feet
To fulfill a maternal task
And bring this child to maturity
And in troubled times to wear a mask
For she cannot be seen to falter
Along life's sometimes bumpy way
Which may allow her offspring
Perhaps to go astray
But ere' long the child is now adult
And decisions that they take
May differ from a Mother's wishes
Causing a heavy heart to ache
But she knows that she would wish the lad
Success in what he may choose
Even though the decision made
Home companionship she may lose
But as long as he's happy and healthy
And living the life he chose
Mum will ever be living in wonder or worry

But deep inside she really knows
That the bond between Mother and child is deep
In thoughts they are never far away
Not even in the time she may sleep
But worry no further dear Mother
In a lads thoughts you are ne'er far away
He knows you are there to support him
Whether in work or in play
So cast care aside, throw your arms open wide
Watch the Sun on your window pane
And save all the love and embraces
Till your Lad's return home once again

Dennis Shrubshall   3rd September 2009

After Dusk

As daylight ends and night descends
The time is drawing nigh
It is time to think of the day that has passed
Now that the moon has appeared in the sky
And reflect on the things that might have been
Were there things that you might have altered
Or would you like once again to relive those hour
To see if on that journey you faltered
Are you happy to forget just another day
In the passage of the Life you chose
For everyone must have a dream
And dreams come true sometimes I suppose
Life is a mystery to everyone
Nobody knows what may happen tomorrow
A Fortune Teller may hazard a guess
It may well be happiness or sorrow
So try if you can to enjoy every day
For the hands of the clock of Life won't turn back
But an abundance of Health and Happiness
Mean more than any finances you may lack
Then when you wake up in the morning
And with boldness you can stride
To face the future with a strong resolve
In that great big world outside .

Dennis Shrubshall   16th May 2009

"Bluffers"

From the time one is born into this world
There is lifelong mystery
Concerning the way a child will grow
And reach their maturity
For Females it is a matter of progression
As from a Girl to a Young Woman they grow
But this doesn't apply to the male of the species
For it takes much longer for them to although
When young they will bounce on their Mother's knee
Perhaps on the floor play with a few toys
Then over the years progression for them means
They're bigger toys for bigger boys
Now this is where comes a twist in the tale
As true story I'm telling unfolds
For it seems that the females will shun these lads
And keep them outside of their strongholds
And then at their leisure the may let them enter
Under surveillance all the time
To make sure just what their intentions are
Are they really little angels sublime
But once the die is cast and unions made
The young ladies seem to be left in some doubt
Have these cheeky chaps answered their questions with
truth
Or is there something they've purposely left out
It is now you may notice there'll be a wind of change
As the lads seem to hedge to & fro

Without a straight answer to the questions they're asked
Which is what the ladies are wanting to know
Excuses run rife as the battle seems lost
Tho' proudly they still battle on
With untruths and a play on sympathy
When they know that all hope has gone
Now that is when they come to the end of the road
Like a locomotive as it hits the buffers
Which unfortunately leaves the male populace
The reputation of a load of old "bluffers".

Dennis Shrubshall   1st November 2009

Dream at Midnight

When you sit alone at night
Recalling events in your mind
It's in the early hours of the morning
When it seems that Fate's been unkind
There seems no one you can turn to
When advice and assurance you need
Although it's been said many times before
A true friend is a friend in deed
There seems no light at the end of the tunnel
Where will your awesome journey end
And suddenly the answer may be before you
Were the words in front of you from a friend
It seemed that your plight had reached a listening ear
And the tears fell like rain as she cried of her plight
And read through the tears words of comfort
As they talked well into the night
In a virtual embrace via the Internet
As this stranger said hold my hand tight
And slowly the loneliness drifted away
From her body was lifted this shroud
And she could see the silver lining
Behind what was a threatening cloud
And slowly she walked to the bedroom
Where she gently on the pillow laid her head
And where the future seemed bleak before her
She now saw life's sunshine instead
And I know that she'll be ever thankful

As she knows that Happiness will again descend
Helped by the hands of a stranger
Her newly found Internet Friend

Dennis Shrubshall   16th December 2010

George

There's a story I'd like to tell you
It happened some years ago
When I was just a novice
And the ropes I didn't know
I'd not long donned the Uniform
To operate as a W P C
In fact a lady policewoman
That's what I wanted to be
When one day whilst on duty
I took a call from a lady in distress
So I took down all the details
With adequate carefulness
The Lady's name and address
Quite clearly noted where
Then joined a waiting patrol car
Which quickly took me there
When I asked what was the problem
I made a note of what she said
I'm worried about my Dear George
I think he's in the Lounge lying dead
So I'd called the Paramedics
Which I thought was right and fair
And they pulled up the same time as us
And one escorted me in there
The worried lady led the way to the Lounge
"Poor George is in there" was what she said
And as we entered the room we saw

On the carpet a Budgie lay dead
So the moral of this story was
If you're with this situation met
Please don't dial the Police on 999
Just phone you local Vet

Dennis Shrubshall   31st December 2011

Harry the Miner

Now Harry was a lovely man
A very good friend to me
So I'll tell you a little story
Then you can plainly see
He stood 6ft 1" in his stockinged feet
A slim yet muscular man
Spent all his days in the bowels of the Earth
Since his working life began
Barely 13 years old when he started work
And down into the pit he was sent
His task was to collect bones from the miners
Remains of children who's lives were spent
Toiling away alongside the Miners
Doing the menial tasks they were set
Before the advent of pit ponies
And a mere few pence would they get
But Harry just went to the pit each day
His "bait" in tin box and Jenny too
For if he wanted a drink during the day
Cold Tea was the best he could do
He'd carry a Pick , a Shovel and a Canary
A Helmet and some Candle stubs too
For these were the recognised tools of the Trade
In the pit where he spent his Life through
But during WW2 he'd have joined the Military
Like all the young men in the crowd
But because he was a "Bevan Boy"

This simply wasn't allowed
Because he'd spent his life in the pit
As Mining was reserved occupation
Instead of becoming a Soldier at War
He was mining for Coal for the Nation
But sometime in the late 50's
A Rescue Worker Harry was made
Where in the event of a disaster
His lifelong experience would be displayed
One terrible day I remember
The Klaxon siren through the village did sound
And all the village women went to the pit
Not a word spoken there was silence all around
There had been a fall in the pit down below
13 men were trapped in there without doubt
When asked about rescue procedure
The Pit Owner said it's too expensive to get the men out
So Harry and his mate fetched a long rope
And Harry was lowered 30 feet down below
Where he found a pit prop had fallen blocking the exit
And into action he had to go
He crawled beneath the Prop and lifted on his shoulders
Without any sign of fear
Which made just enough room as an exit
For his workmates were able to crawl clear
Harry was pulled to the surface
And in silence he walked home
A most harrowing day of his life
To be greeted by his young Granddaughter
And Margaret his ever-loving Wife
The prop had bitten deep into the flesh on his shoulders
The wounds treated by his wife with loving care
And clearly etched the sign on her face
To see Harry standing there
But 2 days passed and he was back on the job
Down to the pit face again
With never a sign of emotion
Nor mention of the physical pain
The Pit Owner learnt what Harry had done
And had a Special Bravery Medal made
To commemorate the saving of 13 lives
And the heroism Harry displayed
He was always a very quiet man

At the end of a shift while walking home he would sing
And when he was ever asked why he would say
The Sky and fresh air are my everything
His only son was never allowed to go near a pit
Nor crawl on his belly underground to feed
Tho' he had spent all those hours underground
It was not for his son he decreed
On his 87th birthday in the Pub he drank and he sang
His favourite song and some may have cried
Then sat in the corner drinking his beer
And that was where he quietly died
His Medal had lain in the drawer unseen
Hidden tribute to a man whose body was scarred and
ingrained
With shoulder that ached every day of his life
And in the N C B's Museum the Medal has remained.

Dennis Shrubshall   24th January 2012

Moving

I've only moved twice in my married life
After much planning and thought
We moved into a new Bungalow
That for £1700. we bought
And after nine years and two children
Our home was only quite small
Just a Bathroom,Kitchen Lounge and 2 Beds
And a narrow nine by three hall
So with bit in my mouth I made the decision
A new Chalet I was going to build
I didn't think there'd be problems
But all the doubts were soon killed
By the Park I picked a site with great care
But when it came to the planning
The Council deemed I should build a pair
The whole of the site they were spanning
The foundations I dug and the concrete I poured
14 hours a day was my task
Then brick after brick I layed with my trowel
Was my target, 2 months, too much to ask
When 4 weeks had passed the walls were all up
And on went the roof rafter by rafter
The Tiles and the floors,the doors and the Plaster
Then the heating and plumbing followed after
The "Sparks" and the Painter add the final touch
We met our goal and I'd like to explain
That as we were finished 39 years ago
I vowed never to move again

Dennis Shrubshall   28th June 2007

Ode to St. Valentine's Day

Have you ever sat and wondered
How a certain day came about
What was it's origination
Was there any reason for doubt
'twas said in the past that it started
In ancient Rome it seems
As a day of celebration
And creating Lover's dreams
On the day before Lupercalia
February the Fourteenth to be exact
But there are many variations
And I'm not sure which is fact
For Claudio 11 the Emperor of Rome
All those many years ago
Cancelled the privilege of Marriage to couples
So that Bachelors to war his soldiers would go
Then 'tis said a certain Saint Valentine
Ignored the rule and couples he still wed
Until Claudio became aware of his actions and announced
"To the dungeons with the scoundrel and off with his
head"
And lo and behold that's what happened
In the cells he was cast to await
Clubbing to death and beheading
Was the sentence to be his fate
Whilst he was waiting to meet his demise
With a sentence so vicious and hard

He wrote his last words to his loved one
Perhaps creating the first Valentine's Card
And it still serves today as a sign of deep affection
To Beaux & Belles of this World far and wide
As a permanent Memorial to Saint Valentine, it's founder
On the 14th of February the day that he died.

Dennis Shrubshall   5th February 2011

Platitude

When sitting alone in contemplation
Do you close your eyes too as tho' asleep
Reflecting perhaps on the past in your life
The fond Memories you will always keep
But when you reflect on those bygone days
Do you also remember with ire
The temper and tumult within your soul
Which burnt like a consuming fire
In times when anger took over
Vitriol and malice seemed to run rife
As though tearing the heart from your body
Transforming to a hateful outlook on life
For it seems now and then that the Demons take over
And wreak havoc from deep within
Turning your once ever tranquil being
To commit every conceivable sin
And never did you consider the fault to be yours
As you continued to rant and rave
Not really a prime example of guidance
If teaching a Family how to behave
But always after what may be termed as outbursts
And your own gentle soul returned
You knew in your heart there must be a solution
Maybe many a lesson to be learned
Then examined with thought and deliberation
Putting these angry episodes through a virtual sieve
Perhaps 'tis better to speak your mind without grudge
And find the platitude to forgive

Dennis Shrubshall   22nd January 2010

Racing Car Driver

Close your eyes for a minute and think
Back to the days as a Lad
You'd dream of the things you'd like to be
Or maybe just follow your Dad
A Pilot, A Soldier or a Fireman
Or a Sailor out on the open Sea
But for some it's a Racing Driver
Combined with the thrills of the Grand Prix
To sit in the seat in your suit of White
Adorned by a helmet too
Waiting to close the visor
When all the preliminary tasks are through
Now you're finally lined up on the grid
The Starter standing still and steady
Before he lowers the flag
When he knows that you are all ready
Now the flag is down is down and the race is on
And as one the magnificent cars their engines roar loud
Joined by the smell of burnt rubbers and fumes
And the excitement of the watching crowd
Each driver doing his level best
To maintain the ultimate speed
To overcome all other opponents
In the hope that they might succeed
And stand there on the winners podium
Wearing the winners wreath
And showering his worthy rivals for the honour

With Champagne as they stand on the level beneath
Now the race is in full swing as they jostle for position
Ready to take any available chance
To pass the cars in front of them
And maybe their final position enhance
Power down the straight then corner wide
Taking the chiquane at top speed
All inhibitions trying to hide
Lap after lap increasing the lead
In the end each second may be important
If in pit stops time is lost
Always on the mind of the driver
As he knows what may be the ultimate cost
Lap after lap and the tension mounts
Spectators are all getting excited
When all of a sudden a driver loses control
His car hits the barrier ,turns over and is ignited
But the cars race on oblivious to the danger
For their goal is now within sight
Any loss of concentration could prejudice their result
If they worry of their fellow drivers plight
But the danger's passed now and the crashed driver is free
And the Marshals have finished their task
The blazing vehicle is extinguished without loss of life
Not much more could anyone ask
Now they're into the final lap now
Competition is up to a fever pitch now
The 2 leading drivers throw caution to the wind
To be first across the line somehow
The crowd all now stand as the chequered flag is dropped
And wonder how this race will end
Maybe the two cars were so close at the finish
That on a photo it will all depend

Dennis Shrubshall   3rd May 2012

Silent prayer

I stopped outside the Church
In our local Town at the end of the Market Square
And I noticed a young woman who walked through those
doors
And on her face I noticed a look of despair
So after a few minutes I too walked into Church
And quietly closed the doors behind
There was this solitary figure head bowed on her knees in
silence
And I wondered just what was on her mind
I sat and I pondered the possibilities and reasons for her
visit
What had brought about this look of despair
Then after a while she rose to her feet
And passed me as she left
The worries on her face no longer there
Then as I was leaving the Padre came along
And of my reasons I made him aware
It was then he explained the young Lady had lost a loved
one
And found solace and comfort in silent prayer

Dennis Shrubshall   8th September 2011

The Blacksmith

On the edge of the rural community
The village Smithy stands
Manned by the local Blacksmith
Recognised by his sturdy hands
Strengthened each day by the hammer he wields
Shaping steel on the Anvil each day
Working the bellows on the furnace
Then with white hot steel he will flay
With his hammer against the Anvil
To flatten or shape or point
Or maybe to make a hinge –pin
To form a movable joint
On which to hang a five barred gate
To a house or a field maybe
Every day his task is different
He enjoys a life of variety
People come from far and wide
To see him ply the skills of his trade
Preceded by his Ancestors most likely
Going back many a decade
He may be asked to forge a tool
Of a customers design
Maybe make some iron keepsakes
When he ever has spare time
But one of his most important tasks
For his local Equestrian friends
Is to fashion some new horseshoes

Which on his Anvil he bends
After which he'll become the Farrier
Taking care of a horse that's thrown a shoe
You'll see the dedication in his face
As he gains the Horse's confidance too
With hoof held firm between his legs
As he tries the shoe for size
Then he heats it again in the furnace for fitting
And when placed you'll see smoke rise
Then adeptly with his hammer
The necessary nails are now in place
Then snipped and filed ands hoof is polished
Once more a smile on the Horseman's face
Then the Smithy will stroke the horse's head
And bid the equestrian pair farewell
Wondering what tomorrow may bring
A Blacksmith can never tell

Dennis Shrubshall   27th September 2011

The Leaves of Autumn

The morning Sun is rising now
Another day to start
Yet another Summer is leaving soon
And those halcyon days will depart
So too the fragrance of Flowers in bloom
And trees and shrubs an abundance of Green
Giving way to the changing Seasons
And a welcome to the Autumn scene
Leaves are now beginning to fall
Blossoms have bloomed now fade and die
The Sun is seen less frequently now
Often shrouded by clouds in the sky
Then as you walk along in the countryside
The trees are changing from green to Gold
Or varying shades of Russet, Tan or Red
A wondrous sight to behold
With a cooling breeze to aid their fall
Myriads of leaves form a carpet on the ground
Natures cloak of many variegated colours
At the foot of the trees will be found
Now is the task of the gardener
Which Flowers and plants shall he save
For some seem to cope with the Winter quite well
Mother Nature's taught them how to behave
But for others they have to be raised and stored
To be planted again next Spring
Protected from ravages of wet and cold

So that in Summer their praises we'll sing
It's time to prune shrubs and trees now
Trim the lawn and cut back the hedges too
And use the Secateurs on the Roses
To encourage new growth to show through
It's also time to dig over the flower beds
Let them lie in the Winter fallow
Covered by a layer of shredded bark
After planting some Tulips and Daffodils shallow
Remove all the plants from the Greenhouse
After turning the soil just once more
Perhaps treat the inside with Jeyes fluid
To rid of garden pests for sure
Then it's away to the shed
For the Mower Fork and Spade
The Shears Hoe and the Tine rake too
Then retire indoors until next Spring
When there'll be plenty of chores once again to do

Dennis Shrubshall   30th October 2010

The Tuskegee Airmen

The thrill of a life as a Flyer
Always many a young lads dream
Only available to the elite
A remote career it would seem
But not so in much Wartime
When many young Servicemen are sought
The Army , Navy and Air Force
The country's enemies to thwart
And this was the case in World War 2
With young men from the U S of A
Were involved in the battle to survive
Both at home and in lands far away
So the tale I'll tell is of "The Tuskegee Airmen"
The name by which they became known
The all-black 332nd Fighter Group
Who earned a Distinguished Unit Citation of their own
They flew a flight of P-51 Mustangs
Colonel Benjamin Davis was their Officer in charge
Their mission to protect B 17 Bombers on a raid
And keep the Messerschmitt 163 & 262's at large
The Bomber force had a target that day
The Daimler Benz Tank factory in Berlin
Charles Brantley, Earl Lane & Roscoe Brown
Shooting down German Jets as the Bombers begin
Their successful attack to create another blow
To cripple manufacture of machines of war
And carried out further missions like this

Initiating the 477th Bombardment Group in 1944
It was part of the Tuskegee Experiment
To integrate coloured Aviators to B25 Bomber crews
Until they entered the all-white Officers Club
They were charged with mutiny making front page news
Thurgood Marshall represented the officers in court
As they were jailed as a result of confrontation
But all were soon released once again
'cept one guilty of violence and fined for the violation
The unit carried on after the cessation of war
And The Army Air Corps the U S Air Force became
Along with a Tuskegee Pilot
Daniel "Chappie" James Jr. was his name
He flew in Korea and then in Vietnam
Then moved to Wheelus Air Base in Tripoli
Where he was then Officer in Command
For a Brigadier General was he
As was Benjamin O Davis Jr the first coloured General
And Lucius Theus at Major General making three
This story has been told many times I expect
To relate Heroic stories never fails
And I'm told this story was one of great appeal
And appears in the Movie called "Red Tails"

Dennis Shrubshall   25th January 2012

Unsung Heroes

To join the Army was my choice
No other career ever on my mind
For I looked forward to seeing the World
For the unusual sights I might find
And once in Uniform I filled with pride
Would the decision I'd made be right
As I served my Queen and Country
Well armed and ready for the fight
Then I served in many theatres of War
Battles fought in a Foreign land
Where Man's brutality to Man
Was difficult to understand
Whilst engaged in conflict you are ever alert
Trying to think the next stage ahead
To avoid the obstacles and booby traps
Or you may be a casualty or even dead
But when perhaps your last Tour is over
And home once again you return
To a Medical Officers examination
Your Mental condition is some cause for concern
And even in the fiercest of battles
Not one injury or wound did you receive
And because your body was void of physical scars
It is difficult for others to conceive
That locked inside the frame of your body
There were Mental scars Oh! so deep
From the atrocities and horrors of Combat

And many for Life you'll have to keep
But sadly now the decision has been made
Your Military Career has come to an end
As you're declared unfit for active duty
No longer able, your Country to defend
It is now that your thoughts you try to gather
What will happen to my future in life
How will I look after my Children
And care for my ever loving Wife
To return to Civilian Life was always difficult
To accept for any ex Military Man
For many had no knowledge of Life outside the Army
Before their Service Life began
So now as you sit indoors and alone
With eyes tightly closed , deep in thought
You witness the slaughter, the noise, smell the Cordite
Of many previous battles you've fought
The cries and screams of men injured by mines
As you stand over their bodies overwrought
For they were your mates at that time of conflict
Together you always fought side by side
But now you silently reflect on those friendships
And honour those colleagues that died
You try to be rational and sort out the turmoil
That repeatedly comes to your mind
Hoping that in the very near future
Someone a solution will find
To end the problems of a Soldier in torment
For his return to a normal life
To enjoy the laughter and play with his children
And the warm caress of his ever loving Wife
But fortunately now there may be help at hand
For many who suffer this condition every day
Such as Combat Stress and other organisations
Tirelessly working PTSD to allay
For many of the victims are our unsung heroes
No Medals or Honours did they seek for the task
They just wish to return to their former life
Is that too much to ask.

Dennis Shrubshall   2nd January 2010

Worry not Mother

Hi Mum now don't you worry
Cos' I'm not home with you
For you're a busy Woman
And there's lots of things for you to do
I knew that when I joined the Army
My former life would change
And giving up Civilian life
At first was rather strange
But all the things you taught me
As I grew up through life
Both Dad as the head of the household
And you the loving Mother and wife
You've still got the girls to look after
And I'm never far away
No matter what I'm doing
You're in my thought each day
Though I know that things have been a bit hard
For me in the last few weeks
Bur perhaps that's really how life is
It has it's "lows" and has it's "peaks"
But I'll do the job that I signed to do
I know that I'll make you proud
As I strive to eventually achieve my goal
Then I can hold my head high in a crowd
But I know it will take some time and thought
And results will not come in a hurry
So here's a big hug and a kiss from me
And Mum whatever you do don't worry.

Dennis Shrubshall   13th October 2009

147

Strange Bedfellows

This is just a little personal story
When Kathy was a teenager no more
At the tender age of twenty years
She travelled to a Foreign shore
She landed in the Islands of New Guinea
A young lady from a Rural town
On a visit to be among the natives
And a Mission of small renown
As a Catholic she was familiar with Nuns and Priests
But here they were in a different guise
No longer dressed in surplice or gown
But in old shorts with mud around their thighs
She was shown to her accommodation
Which was a hut made from the leaves of a palm
Woven together to form walls and the roof
To keep out the rain and shelter from harm
Altho' the hut kept out the weather
Strange creatures it did not exclude
Which were plentiful in this primitive area
Scary for one when in solitude
She'd woken at night to see things there
On the table beside her bed
Not just belongings or water in a glass
But all sorts of creatures instead
But a large size rodent was sitting there beside her
She's never seen one as big as that
Not in her wildest imagination

A rat that was nearly as big as a cat
She imagined what it was thinking
As before it's evil gaze she lay
Would she be the first victim
That this nasty creature would nibble today
All sorts of things went through her head
Whilst she stayed in the rodents glare
How many times had she slept unknowing
Of the creature watching her there
You may ask why didn't she rise and run
Into the open away from the bed
It was because of a damaged and swollen knee
Or she may have upped and fled
So she thought to herself as she grabbed her pillow
Maybe she could take control
Of a situation where she was hostage to a rodent
And then her retribution could extol
Then as she started to lift her arm and swing
Onto the bed the Rat leapt
Running around on top of her as she scream aloud
Waking everyone who may have slept
Then in walked the Priest and said "What's going on"
In a voice that would never fail
To instil any Damsel's confidence
As he grabbed the Rat by the tail
And threw the creature as far as he could
Then escorted young Kathy to the Toilet in the dark
As any Priesthood father would
Akin to any everyday occurrence
Or that is the way that it would appear
Always take control when faced by terror
And never give way to fear

Dennis Shrubshall   4th December 2012

Chickens

I've seen many pets in my life
Though no particular variety comes to mind
When I think of what may have been a favourite
What sort what shape what kind
But of late my thoughts have turned
Away from what others might think
As I look at the fluffy objects I've acquired in a box
That lies open on the Kitchen sink
I fell in love with these tiny creatures
No more than a week into this world
As they nestle beside each other in the hay
With their wings so tightly curled
It was then that it sprang to my mind
What am I going to do with them now
They won't survive in a box for long
I'll have to re-house them somehow
So I bought some timber and made them a coop
With boarding and felt for the roof
Which would keep them safe from predators
And dry from the rain from aloof
I formed a nice exercise area
A timber frame covered with netting of wire
With height that they may stretch their wings
But deter them from flying higher
It was a pleasure to watch them grow from chicks
And watch them surely grow
Fortunately they were female pullets

And not Cockerels with a mighty crow
At least they are safe within their run
Away from predators running wild
Happy within their environment
Although not entirely beguiled
They'll eat their food and run about
Perhaps sometimes eggs they'll lay
Never suspecting their lives may end
When laying eggs they are unable
They might finish up as "Coq au Vin"
Dished up on the Dining Table.

Dennis Shrubshall   25th June 2011

Mountains

The Universe covers Oh! so much
A subject so complex and so vast
So it's time to itemise my thoughts
With memories from the past
I've flown the skies so many times
And high above the earth we soar
Looking at the world beneath us
Different Countries and Oceans and more
But the one thing that always compels me
To reflect on those flights again
Is the sight of the tips and mountain tops
Whether America or Austria or Spain
But because I come from the U S of A
My thoughts will always return
To the Appalachian Mountain Range
For which my heart will always yearn
Starting down in Georgia and up to Pennsylvania
The Blue Ridge Mountains stand
With their bluish haze against the sky atop
Which makes them a spectacular scene so grand
In the valley down below the National Park of Shenandoah
The Great Smoky National Park and Blue Ridge Parkway
too
It is where the visitors come for vacations in their
thousands
As there is so much here that they can do
Sioux Manahoacs, Iroquois and Shawnee

Were the inhabitants of the valley in times now long past
But in the 17th Century when the area was Colonised
The American Indian population diminished quite fast
There are Oak and Hickory forests on the slopes of the Appalachians
Then there is grass , Shrubs and Hemlock and some Oak-pine
The trees there are heaven for myriads of birds
And they all seem to get along quite fine
There's Humming |Birds and Grouse and even wild turkeys too
And running wild is the Boar and the occasional Deer
Where in times now long gone the Indians would be hunting
Not forgetting the Black Bear who was their greatest fear
Now we live in a world where this beauty is preserved
A heritage that's treated with love and care
So that future generations will be able to enjoy
The Blue Ridge Mountains and the lovely mountain air

Dennis Shrubshall　　　　　　　　9th October 2011

"In the Blue Ridge Mountains of Virginia
On the trail of the lonesome Pine
In the pale moonshine our hearts entwine
Where you carved your name and I carved mine."

Marriage

Marriage is not just a Ceremony
Where a loving couple are Wed
It is the start of a lifelong partnership
To span the many years ahead
It usually starts with heads in the clouds
There seems no rain in the sky
But as the months and year roll on
In bliss the time seems to fly
You live in a world together
With very little time spent apart
Everyday deeds and actions and words
Which always come straight from the heart
Then as your life moves slowly forward
For many with Children they are blessed
To form a new Family union
And give this new Challenge a test
With Love and dedication
The youngsters will grow and succeed
A credit to their loving Parents
Their happiness is decreed
But sometimes in life as in all things
Perhaps a little rain may fall
When you're made aware of a threat to your life
And it's then on your inner strength you may call
With the Love of your life there beside you
To fight the problems as only you know how
Enhanced by the love from your Children

Together you're a formidable Army now
So you'll fight this Demon within you
On this battle your life may depend
But with a solid determination
Your troubles will come to an end
Then once again you can forward go
And return to the happiness you once knew
Two contented lovers walking hand in hand
And the Family who helped you see your troubles through

Dennis Shrubshall   26th August 2009

Image of you

Look in the Mirror and what do you see
Is a stranger before your eyes
If you stare ahead with determined look
Is it someone you recognise
Do you watch in despair
As you comb your hair
Perhaps turn your head to one side
Is this the image you saw before
When upset you broke down and cried
Did you feel you could ask for comfort
Perhaps a shoulder to cry on now and again
Did the image in the glass ever change
When you seemed to be in great pain
All these thoughts pass your mind each morning
In the bathroom as you come into view
Are you still looking there at a stranger
And is she still looking at you
Or do you notice there's gradual change day by day
In her eyes can you sense there is love
Or is there divine intervention
From someone watching above
Something has changed in the pattern
And now you can easily tell
That after your tears and worries
You seem to have broken the spell
That bound you and your image in the bathroom
With the person you tried not to be

And now it seems you are you once again
Happy and fancy free
To enjoy your life as you did in the past
Without a worry or care
And you can now stand in front of the mirror
And not see the other image there

Dennis Shrubshall.   30th October 2010.

Henry The Eighth

This tale all started long ago
In the year of Fourteen Ninety One
When Elizabeth of York and Henry the Seventh
Were blessed with a second son
This handsome lad grew from strength to strength
Prince Henry was his name
And by the time he was 22 years old
He was to prove his claim to fame
For at that time a King led his Army into battle
With his trusty Steed, his Sword and Shield
And this was the task of Henry The English leader
In Fifteen Thirteen at the Battle of Flodden Field
A battle to thwart the attack of the Scots and the French
And Ten Thousand Scottish soldiers were slain
Along with their leader James Fourth King of Scotland
But 1500 bodies of English Soldiers at Flodden would
remain
Then his efforts to denounce Martin Luthers ideals
Without the use of his trusty sword
Came to the notice of the Pope at that time
Earning the title "Defender of the Faith" as his reward
He'd proved his worth on the field of conflict
But governing the country to him held no charm
He left most decisions to Cardinal Wolsey , the
Archbishop of York
Preferring to ride with the Hunt on a farm
Catharine of Aragon bore Henry a daughter

Which was not what King Henry had planned
He was hoping she would bear him a Son and heir
Perhaps sometime to help him rule this land
But this marriage was never deemed to last
A fact that was plain to see
And without much help from Cardinal Wolsey
Divorced Catherine in Fifteen Thirty Three
Henry then married Anne Boleyn
Although heavily pregnant was she
She then bore him a Daughter Elizabeth
And met her demise when beheaded for infidelity
Once again he was married by the end of the month
And Jane Seymour became his blushing Bride
But sadly in giving birth to his son and heir Edward
This unfortunate young lady died
Then 4 years passed and Henry arranged another
marriage
A German Princess and Anne of Cleves was her name
But this happy union was never consummated
No mention was made as to who was to blame
In July 1540 Henry married Catherine Howard
They were happy or so it would seem
But two years later something happened between them
To shatter this Royal dream
Catherine was accused of having an illicit affair
An adulterous wife or so it was said
Henry had her locked up in the Tower and executed
Yet a second of his wives to lose their head
When at last King Henry settled down in 1543
Catherine Parr became his 6th and final wife
She looked after the King and his children
For four years until the end of his life
In his period as King of England
He brought a lot of change in his reign
As head of the Church of England
He cut the English ties Rome and the Pope once again
Overseeing the dissolution of the Monastries
Instituting changes in Religion and governing of Law
Which lasted a100 years until the death of Charles the 1st
And the Commonwealth was established for evermore.

Dennis Shrubshall   24th January 2011

Free Spirit

Oh! to be a free spirit
For the world is your oyster you know
Your presence is seen and felt each day
Wherever you may go
Nobody can take what you hold dear
Loving heart and a mind that's free
Of acrimony and vitriol
Mistress of your destiny
Never afraid to state your case
And hope solutions are close at hand
Help is available from your friends
Always ready to listen and understand
You pretend and see and want what you are
Maybe worry and touch and dream
Aim for the ultimate goal in your life
Though sometimes impossible it may seem
Now if you add all these things together
And I'm sure you are going to
The most important thing to remember forever
Is that you will always be you.

Dennis Shrubshall   15th May 2010

Enlistment

In teenage life it was Oh! too plain
To be a Soldier I was very keen
Was I prepared to spend my Life
In the Service of the Country and the Queen
The options of employment were varied
As a mechanic or a mediocre Office Clerk
Drive a Bus or a Train or join the Navy
Perhaps the Local Council cutting grass in the Park
But my mind was set and I wouldn't budge an inch
And for Mum & Dad the news came hard
As this was the time for the parting of the ways
And the Home life that I'd known I must discard
Then it was down to the local Railway Station
With my case of belongings suitably packed
So with a handshake from my Dad
And, from Mum a kiss last embrace
To hide the tears I turned so quickly
That I nearly dropped my case
But once the journey to the Training Camp had ended
I was mixing with lads who joined like me
The loneliness that I was feeling soon departed
With some friendly patter and joviality
Next morning was revelation
As the Sergeant came into the Barrack room at dawn
It's six oclock and time for Breakfast
Then down to the Barber's to get you heads shorn
Then on to the Stores for uniforms 2

And kitbag, Haversack and Backpack
Eating Irons, Tea mug , Bed Linen
Blankets and Cherry Blossom boot polish Black
The buttons now are Everbright
Cuts out the cleaning of Brass
But you still "bull" your boots and clean your Rifle
Ever keen to stay top of the class
Out on the Square you march till you drop
Then down to the Gym for some P T
And by the time you sit down for dinner
Military life you're beginning to see
Then it's down to the classroom for Technical training
Followed by a stint on the Firing Range
To get you used to the noise of a discharge
And how fast the cartridges you can change
It's two months of intensive training, now ended
And a Trade you will now need to choose
Be it Tanks or Guns and Artillery, or Technical
Or an Officers Batman and learn to shine shoes
And once you have passed the various Trade Tests
Wearing your Uniform with pride
You will no doubt receive your first Posting
In the U K or maybe worldwide
For this is the time you have waited for
As the Soldier you always wanted to be
And be part of a Professional Fighting force
At Home or over the Sea
To a far flung land many miles from home
To a Jungle swamp or Desert Oasis maybe
During the course of your Service Life
Against Oppression, Terrorism or Hostility
But the training you had was the best in the World
And instant reaction to the word of Command
For your Life or others may depend on the speed you act
And caution too, your Officer will demand
So as the years pass by so slowly at first
You may wonder if you made the right choice
Then when you get leave to return to your home
Your Parents and Family will rejoice
There's no doubt there's some danger involved in the life of
a Soldier
Than driving a Bus or a Tractor or a Train
But the fact that you are living your dream

Will outweigh that again and again
So forward go and strive to attain
To reach the top by promotion with every stride
And the rewards you receive by your efforts
Will be balanced by your Personal Pride
For a job well done in any walk of life
As a Military man or any other
To succeed in the life you chose will win esteem
From a very proud Father and Mother.

Dennis Shrubshall   5th September 2009

Chit Chat

Sitting at home with an open mind
Of the fun with the people I've met
Since I dared enter those Hallowed Halls
In the Chat Room on the Internet
A band of virtual Brothers and Sisters
Or virtual Mum's or Dad's to some
Especially to Ladies of lesser years
When into the company they first come
For the ages are so varied
Without bias to Women or Men
And the Ladies can give as good as they get
When they're tormented now and then
It's nice to sit and watch as they chat
About places far and wide
And noticeable too for some first timers
When inhibitions they try to hide
For it's a way to spend an hour or two
In some friendly banter or chat
And if anyone gets a bit out of order
We soon put a stop to that
There's many a laugh and sometimes a tear
For a sad moment of the past
But never the time to dwell on sorrow
As the conversations are going quite fast
Sometimes you can see who you're talking to
If the Webcam is switched on
Especially when their image is frozen

And you know that the owner has gone
You can have a chat in private
Where addresses you are able to exchange a treat
Yet retain your confidentiality
And unwanted viewer you defeat
For me it opened a new way of leisure
In new avenues I started to look
Then I learned about the lives of some of the Ladies
And wrote it down in verse and entered them into my book
So I'd like to advise those people who've not tried it
To give it a go as on numbers it depends
And maybe , like me you'll enjoy the good company
Of a host of Internet Friends.

Dennis Shrubshall   26th July 2009

Artistic Gardens

Overhead the clouds are floating
Like a blanket of white in the sky
Interspaced here and there with patches of blue
As slowly they pass us by
The wind is blowing a gentle breeze
In which the trees seem to bend
Ever aware that if the wind should cease
Rain from the clouds would descend
On our ever thirsty gardens
Awaiting a Summer shower
So gently it falls and fresh is the scent
On the shrubs and every welcoming flower
Saving the gardener just one of his chores
To keep them with water supplied
For he knows the serious consequences
Of the plants, if of moisture they are denied
All this can be seen as round the garden you stroll
Admiring the beautiful view
Creating a colourful Floral image
As most well-kept gardens do
Do you think sometimes of a gardener as an artist
As with care he arranges plants and flowers in beds
Is he painting with the vibrants and pastels
Of myriads of flowers with variegated coloured heads
For some that I've seen make me sit back and think
Of the amount of thought and planning there displayed
And the care and dedication of the horticulturist

As he plies his knowledge of the trade
Green fingers and love of the garden are essential
If good results you aim to achieve
But now as the Sun sinks the flowers close their heads
And it's once again time for me to leave

Dennis Shrubshall   13th June 2010

Angler's Delight

The beach lies perfect like a golden carpet
Not a ripple to be seen
A vast expanse washed by the tide
A view of cleanliness pristine
Overhead the gulls are winging
Giving out their mournful cry
Ever searching for a tasty morsel
Thrown by a sympathetic passer- by
Boats at moorings now left aground
Rusting chains and buoys abound
Seen by the diggers with forks in hand
Trying to unearth worm bait from the sand
To satisfy the anglers wish
As on the next tide he hopes to find fish
On the safety of his trusty boat
Which once more on the rising water
Will soon safely float
Propelled again to a favourite spot
And then at anchor ride
Waiting to see what Neptune brings
On the ever rising tide
For a vast selection of fish lies hidden
From the eager Anglers eye
As he casts his bait to the open water
And sometimes wonders why
His efforts are unsuccessful
While others catch with every cast

And then his luck has quickly changed
As he reels in his catches quite fast
But he knows too well when the tide has turned
And the waters start to recede
Gone are his chances of catching fish
As they are now off the feed
So he reels in the line and stows the tackle
Starts the engine and heads for the shore
Where he'll secure the boat to the mooring
His fishing trip is over once more

Dennis Shrubshall   18th May 2010

A reason to write

Allen the words I write are simple
The subject matter vast
Images many I portray
About the present and the past
But I know that there are some
With memories they like to keep
Thoughts of friends departed
In the daytime and when they sleep
Suddenly crossed my mind to write some words
That may comfort a troubled mind
So I added an Angel and memorial thought
And mentioned the "footsteps left behind"
But now as I think in retrospect
If I'd thought deeper and with more care
Perhaps I should have forgotten Memories and Angels
But how do I write about a silent prayer.

Dennis Shrubshall

A Fair wind is Blowing

Think back to those days not long ago
When happiness prevailed
And you rode on the wave of Life's ocean
On the ship of Love you sailed
The sky above was cloudless
The water a sparkling blue
And then the world was your oyster
Out there and waiting for you
But the path of life is not quite the same
With many a twist and a turn
And it is only as we grow older
There are frailties that we learn
Which are there it seems to taint the joys
That you and your Family once knew
Though it's hard at times to realize
The way to see the problems through
That's the hand that you've now been dealt
In this game of Life you're playing
Can only be handled with love and compassion
And I know it goes without saying
That they're both there in abundance
And perhaps to set you free
From the sadness that is within you
About the Member of your Family
So open wide the windows
Of this sad and lonely room
Which brings you this anxiety

Full of sorrow and gloom
Unlock these doors of misery
With arms wide and an open heart
And enjoy the Spring and the flowers in bloom
To welcome to your world a new start
Encourage some happiness back into your life
At the end of that tunnel is light
A solution to your problems is waiting for you
Not far away but out of sight
The decisions you made were hard ones
To bring to the end the pain
And now with your growing confidence
They'll soon be walking again
So look boldly again to the future
Erase sadness and sorrow from your mind
And you'll sail again on Life's Ocean
And leave your troubles in the wake behind.

Dennis Shrubshall   3rd April 2009

Butterflies

Mother Nature has many creations
On the land and in the Sky
Some so infinitesimal
To be seen with the naked eye
We're surrounded by plants and flowers
Vibrant colours and shade of green
Her beauty is all around us
Waiting to be seen
In the hedgerows there are birds that chirrup away
And others soaring high into the Sky
All sorts of creatures running around
A pleasure to the human eye
But if we care to look closer
At the foliage as we pass
We may see signs of life creating
Not too far above the grass
Eggs have been carefully laid and hidden
And the leaves around them seem to curl
Giving them safety whilst they are growing
And the wonders of Mother Nature unfurl
And after a period of 5 or 6 days
The recent eggs into larvae have grown
And eat their way to the outside of the leaves
On which they eat to survive alone
And after some time it spins it's own web
Covering itself as tho' to hide
Until it faces the world as a chrysalis

To a life in the world outside
Where soon it sheds it's scaly shell
And a few weeks go flying by
Before witnessing the transformation
Into a beautiful Butterfly
With colours in range like a Rainbow
In every conceivable hue
Mother Nature's beautiful creation
For the likes of me and you

Dennis Shrubshall   29th December 2011

Our Puppy

Long long ago or so its seems
My wife decided she's like a pet
So we studied all the advertisements
So see if there was a Puppy we could get
For sale there were plenty of Poodles
And Afghan Hounds and Dachshunds too
There were Yorkie's, & Westie's & Jack Russell'
Border Collies & Labrador's to mention but a few
We saw Chi Hua Hua's & Staffords & Rottweiller's
It would be hard for a choice to for us to make
But to have a Mastiff or a Greyhound or a Retriever
Might prove to be an expensive mistake
We looked at Boxers & Whippets & Dalmations
A Llasa Apso and a Pinscher as well
How could we choose one from all of these dogs
A decision would be difficult I could tell
Then all of a sudden our minds were made up
When a German Shepherd Dog we espied
And then as tho' in a dream it happened
The Alsation Puppy came and stood by our side
It didn't take long to make up our mind
That this was the dog we would choose
We couldn't go home and leave him behind
And the opportunity we dare not lose
The deal was done and he was now our pet
And as he looked up as we walked to the car
We knew that we'd made the right choice

For we'd studied dogs from near and far
He settled in quite nicely for a Puppy
Although to leave the litter was a shame
But his closeness to us made up for that
We decided Shadow would be his name
He'd do the things that all dogs do
Like sit and offer his paw
Or run off up the garden with a slipper
Even "pee'd on the Kitchen floor
But this was the friend that we wanted
As company when my wife was alone
Although a gentle natured dog was he
Unwanted strangers may have entered a war zone
The years came and went but he still seemed the same
Instinctively knew the times for a walk
And would stride by your side very proudly
Only impatient if you stopped for a talk
As he knew in the park he would always run free
And chase after a ball for evermore
Then after a gentle stroll back home
Would collapse in his basket on the floor
But the years take their toll in this life that we live
And for pets age catches up with them just the same
When no longer will they race to the door for a walk
Or go to the park for game
But still they give comfort to their owners
Ever eager to sit by their side
Still keen to have their head stroked
But their tiredness and pain they seem to hide
For they cannot tell you what ails them
As that is all down to your good friend the Vet
Whose task has been to keep the dog in good health
With kindness that you never forget
So it's time now to remember those halcyon days
When Shadow was in his prime
And the happiness and joy that came with him
When you met for the very first time
But no-one can take the memories you hold
They are yours for evermore
And remain very special in your life
After Shadow, for the last time, goes through the door

Dennis Shrubshall   5th January 2011

Melodious Intent

So listen to the rhythm of the falling rain
And see if therein a message lies
For the gentle tip tap on the window pane
Which you can readily melodise
And add the words you want to hear
Come forth to you once again
And you have now created a Ballad
The Rhythm of the Falling Rain
For this is surely one method
Of how songs come to start
And depict our innermost feelings
Or matters of the heart
Wherein we may soar above the clouds
Or merely float on the crest of a wave
But sometimes wallow in a mire
Strange how our minds behave
Not really knowing which way to turn
For 'tis all written in the book of life
Experience is the way to learn
How we overcome trouble and strife
To identify your inner desires
To choose which path is right
Then you can sit at your friendly computer
And compose love songs all through the night.

Dennis Shrubshall   20th January 2008

Road to Romance

Two young people so in love
Oblivious to all around
Each entwined in the others life
Is happiness what they've found
Each waking moment when they're apart
The young lady with stars in her eyes
Taking her loved one into her heart
Hoping he too will realise
For love is determined in so many ways
Sometimes involves give and take
Say the wrong word at the wrong time
And surely a heart may break
Although 'tis said words spoken in haste
May sometimes bring cause for regret
When all it would have taken was a little more thought
Avoiding tears and cheeks that were wet
But alas it can happen too often
For many are guilty as we all know
Releasing wrath out of frustration
Promoting acrimony to grow
But romantics have an inbuilt buffer system it seems
Where tolerance sometimes plays a part
To discuss any difference between them
And heal many a broken heart
But surely this is how love should really be
In what some call the Mating Game
Accepting at times when one is at fault

And agreeing to share some of the blame
For the Path of Live is never straight
Sometimes it may be winding and bending
But as the happy couple stroll the course
Hoping for Fairy Tale ending.

Dennis Shrubshall   28th June 2011

The Gardeners Enemy

This young lady's a bit upset
At what she's seen outside
That all the work she put into the flower bed
Has apparently withered and died
But now this female slouth
With magnifying glass at the ready to hand
Looking for a reasonable answer to why
Her plants met their demise un-planned
Maybe caused by the nasty garden pests
But now she's seen the give away trails
Of Mother natures enemies
Those horrible slugs and snails
So into the shed for the solution
For she'll not let this matter rest
Then sprinkle a generous helping of Slug Pellets
To get rid of her unseen garden pest
Then once more plant the flower beds
With young seedlings anew
And hope that all her efforts
Will bring the Flowers smiling through .

Dennis Shrubshall   8th September 2010

The Long Day

World War 2 had come to a climax
The time for retribution was nigh
With thousands of ships across the English Channel
And thousands of planes in the sky
This was to be a concerted effort
To end the horrendous German reign
Of Nazism with it's killing and slaughter
Then bring peace to Europe once again
So now that the waiting was over
The South of England had Troops everywhere
With all the lanes full of Tanks and Lorries and Artillery
Hidden from observation from the air
The railway yards and docks , the ships and the barges
All with their deadly cargoes concealed
Personnel all sworn to silence
And to no-one was the destination revealed
The decision was made and the convoy left Harbour
Each ship was packed to the"gunnel's"
With Troops and Vehicles and Armourments
In the rough seas poured heavy smoke from their funnels
And over head was a constant roar from the planes
As they droned under their heavy load
On their way to the distant objective
Where the deadly cargo they carried would explode
To pave the way for the seaborne attack
As this enormous Armada the Normandy coast neared
To face an indomitable resistance

Far worse than anyone had feared
Ships were lost and Landing craft too
So near to the target they sought
And the armour and the troops that they carried
For them their last battle was fought
But the battle continued and advances were made
With the German Army in a rapid retreat
For they never expected retaliation, in such great numbers
To bring about their eventual defeat
As we reflect on that day, Oh! so long ago
For some it is hard to believe
The cost in young lives to fight oppression
In order that Peace you may achieve
As you look in the eyes of the few survivors left
On the beaches where their mates all fell
You will still see the compassion and comradeship
That they shared on that D Day of hell
And now as the Last Post is sounded
They close their eyes and they silently pray
Hoping that the World will never forget
Those who laid down their lives on that day

Dennis Shrubshall   7th June 2009.

Time to Reflect.

Have you ever wished that the hands of time
On the clock of Life would stand still
Would you want to return to a bygone day
An event , perhaps, that gave you a thrill
Were you standing on the Parade Ground
When the C.O announced your name
With your head held high, did you proudly march
As to the Presentation Podium you came
The Commendation, aloud was read
For your Comrades all to hear
How you excelled yourself on the battlefield
Although not without some fear
As you carried out your daunting task
Of the British Soldier true and bold
Without the thought that perhaps one day
Your heroic story would be told
In front of the Parade , at attention and with pride
As the C O pins the Medal from his hand
Did you reflect on the comrades and the mates who had died
In that far off Foreign Land.

Dennis Shrubshall   10th December 2008

Wings of an Angel

Oh! that I had the wings of an Angel
Soaring through the sky
Or riding the beautiful cloud formation
Drifting through the heavens so high
In a world so free from worry
Nowhere the sign of despair
I wonder how you qualify as an Angel
And maybe join her there
For her the heavens are open
An area Oh! so vast
And maybe change from cloud to cloud
As they so quickly passed
Surveying all below her
While the rest of the world may sleep
For hers is the task of comforting others
As her heavenly watch she'll keep

Dennis Shrubshall   1st July 2012

TIME

From the *TIME* we are born
To the day that we die
The hands of *Time* go flying by
As Babe's in cradles
Impatiently awaiting their feed
To young Children in class
Who'll gain the experience they need
There's a *TIME* to work
To sleep, eat and learn
And we are ever aware
That each corner we turn
May show a *TIME* to laugh
Or in sadness *TIME* to cry
But there's *TIME* of caution
When we pause for thought
If the *TIME* spent in study
All the right answers have brought
To a mind ever keen
All the avenues to explore
In a never-ending quest for Knowledge
Questions answered by the score
Not all solutions are stored in volumes
On Library shelves gathering dust
But learned from our Elders who
When their Memories are jogged, might just
Recall the information required
Perhaps the date and venue too

On Historical events from the past
Extreme Mathematics or Animals seen in a Zoo
For Life is comprehensive
And a wealth of knowledge sublime
For who knows if we hadn't gained it
What would we have done with all that **TIME**.

Dennis Shrubshall   28th November 2009.

Rambling

Oh! how I long for the countryside
For solitude and peace
A place of pleasant sanctuary
Where worries seem to cease
For here I can bare my very soul
In perfect dignity
Away from all of the strangers
And the only critic is me
I stroll along the country lanes
Until a style I see
A place for entry to the fields beyond
In the world where I long to be
Far away from the towns and cities
The traffic, the hustle, the noise
Here is my Utopia
Where we used to play as boys
Looking out across the hills
When the Sun is coming to rest
Displaying a carpet of green and gold
Before the Twilight that I love best
There's oats & barley & maize and wheat
For Harvest time is here
The time when labourers work from dawn to dusk
To make sure the fields are clear
Then straightaway out with the Tractor and Plough
And till the land for next year
As I'm wandering now past the Farm House

I'm invited in by the Farmer and his Wife
To join them for Supper and a glass of Cider
It's a custom in country life
When I take my leave and stroll along
In the last of the daylight hours
I hear the birds in evening song
As surroundings my eyes scours
I see the run of the wily Fox
The hoot of the Barn Owl from a tree
It seems as though they are putting on a show
Especially for me
And that's why I walk my solitary path
The animals are my company

Dennis Shrubshall   2nd September 2008

Promenade

Strolling the Promenade
In the midst of Winter
No Holidaymakers in sight
What are the thoughts that go thro' your head
Is this the place to live , despite
The fact that so many strangers
In a few more months may choose
To follow in these very footsteps
In an attempt to be rid of the "Blues"
The downside of their everyday life
Their trials and tribulations
Which appear these days to be rife
But they may have chosen this walk, early morning
With nothing particular in mind
And just to breath the fresh Seaside air
Leaving their troubles behind
Then sit in a seafront shelter, facing seaward
And stare at the horizon afar
Catch a sight of the ships that are passing, in the distance
Or the buoys that may mark a sand bar
Away to the left the Estuary and the Lighthouse
With it's ever welcoming light
Like a guiding star to a Mariner
Who may be sailing home by night
But here in the early morning
The fishing boats are leaving the shore
To search the seas for the shoals of fish

Which may fill their trawls once more
Then as tho' by the touch of a switch
Myriads of sails seem to come into view
With the Wind driving all these tiny sailing boats forward
And manned by their 2 man crew
Now it's time to get up and stroll once again
It's just turned ten minutes to eight
Time to return the way that they came
And insure that for breakfast they're not late
It's at times like this that you realise
And it's Oh! so plain to see
That Life has so many joys and pleasures to offer
And surprisingly, of cost, they are free .

Dennis Shrubshall   6th February 2009

Pets

'tis written in the book of life
The dog is the man's best friend
But if you take one for a pet
Where will it all end
The next thing you know
There' a cat in the house
Ready to pounce
On an unsuspecting mouse
Which into the house
Did accidentally stray
Not knowing there was a puss
Waiting for a game to play
So out in the garden
A rabbit hutch erected
To hold another pet or two
In case the others are rejected
But why just have a rabbit
Have a guinea pig ,so meak
And before the day is out
You'll get used to the perpetual squeak
Then when it gets to Summer
And holidays you plan
Don't give a thought to all your pets
Just take them round to Grandad & Nan

Dennis Shrubshall   August 2008

191

My Home

I've lived in Essex for Fifty years now
Oh! how the time seems to fly
Since I moved to the village of Benfleet
To give country living a try
But over the years things have changed so much
From an Urban District to a Borough has grown
When a Bungalow cost a mere £1700 then
But would now cost £200,000- to own
And with the change village life has gone
The shops in the High Street are now few
For most people travel to the Supermarkets
When their weekly shopping they do
But although I was born in the East End of London
I know that I could never return
To the Cosmopolitan jungle that was my birthplace
No matter how much for my Heritage I yearn
So it's here in Essex that I raised my Family
And together we've witnessed Happiness and tears
And I can say without fear of contradiction
It's here I 'll stay and live out the rest of my years

Dennis Shrubshall   17th January 2010

Lovers Tryst

Two people walking hand in hand
Oblivious to the world around
Staring into each other's eyes
In their own little wonderland
And this is perhaps how true love begins
A young couple totally unaware
Of what is all around them
Nor do they seem to care
As they stroll along together
Under a clear blue sky
Without a thought of present events
They don't even seem to try
To break from this magical spell that they're under
In their own little world they seem to live
They are in their own Utopia
In the knowledge the world will forgive
Two people in their own little heaven
Their worries they've left far behind
With singular thoughts and a warm embrace
Hoping that happiness they'll find
For sadly we live in a world today
With compassion and love seldom found
Ever hopeful once again we will live in peace
Where happiness and joy will abound
So we'll wave farewell as our young lovers continue
Down lovers lane that they seem to know well
And trust that their hopes and dreams are fulfilled
But, alas , only time will tell

Dennis Shrubshall   24th June 2010

Looking back

As you lay in repose upon your bed
And gently close your eyes
How many thoughts are going through your head
What do you visualize
Are you thinking back to the early days
Perhaps a hint of your first romance
When you made quick decisions
Not worried about taking a chance
When life you always lived to the full
Although with thought and devotion
But sometimes the snags brought heartache
And an outward show of emotion
Then as the tears had dried upon your cheeks
That relieved the anger and the pain
You realized your inner strength
Had come to your aid again
But also whilst you're thinking back
To the moments that cause you stress
Some fault may lie within yourself
And perhaps creates some bitterness
For you know that now and then maybe
Decisions you've made in vain
Without thought for the repercussions
The sadness and distain
But bold you must be if change you wish
To the way of life you live
You may even when the Demons you find

Realise that they are willing to forgive
Some of your indiscretions or errors you've made
Which may have been with some doubt
And as your life begins to alter
Is the time when you will find out
That it is fallacy to have implicit faith
Without some solid indication
That some of the friends you've singled out
Perhaps will be your salvation
Whilst you stay strong in body and soul
The Devil can try his best
But adversity is always a motivation
To bring your troubles to rest
And then you can open your arms out wide
And all your true friends embrace
As you sail again on Life's ocean
And your foes and troubles sink without trace .

Dennis Shrubshall   25th July 2009

Friendship

And yet another year has gone
So an email says today
Subscription time is here again
It's time for me an annual fee to pay
And so I sit and ponder
Will this facility I use
Or shall I be a free Member
So Poetic friends I don't lose
An answer tho' not hard to find
It's always plain to see
You have to pay for what you want in life
Very little comes for free
Which leads me on to friendship
Abundant here on this thread
Where we can laugh and joke in rhyme
Or be serious instead
The latest news that I've noticed
Ron's working life's expired
So it would be very nice to know
What he's doing now he's retired
It must be nice to know Ron
That this thread long ago was light-hearted
Continues strong in here today
With 29,000 viewers since you first started
So it must still be of interest
To the many who come in daily to look
Or is that perhaps they'll find

The release date of my **new book**
Which I'm pleased to say will be any day now
From the Printers I'm advised
With a fervent hope of it's success
And the Military Charities further subsidised
By generosity from eager readers
For not only can they enjoy the reading
The book **" A Tapestry of Verse"**
Will they help this venture succeeding
The one thing that I'd like to stress
To potential buyers that I've never met
That all **proceeds go to Military Charities**
And not one penny will I get
But then again I've had the pleasure
Writing word by word and line by line
To help someone less fortunate
And to me that sounds just fine
For in the world we live today
A saying that I think is fair
With Health & Friends & Happiness
Without doubt you're a Millionaire

Dennis Shrubshall   4th March 2009

Dementia

In this world there's one thing certain
We all have only one Mother
And she's the one with love endowed
And has shared it with us like no other
When as a child she'd comfort you
And knew the right things to say
Even when you fell and hurt yourself
Whilst you were out at play
But for you and your Mum the time has come
When your roles are now reversed
You are faced with a worrying task
As Mum needs comforting or be nursed
To those outside it appears their lives
Are now spent in a prison cell
But when you visit and hold her hand
It's then that you know too well
That Mum is now in a world of her own
Like you as a girl used to be
Acting out your childhood fantasies
That nobody else could see
So try to set all logic aside
Although I know it's hard
And try to see your Mum as a child again
Playing in her own personal yard
Give her the treats that you know she likes
Chocolates and Flowers I guess
And watch carefully the look upon her face

Totally free from worry or stress
For she's in her second childhood
Her welfare is your main concern
Ever hopeful that a miracle could happen
And the Mum that you knew could return.

Dennis Shrubshall   22nd August 2011

Cats Eyes

Thinking of a cats and the things that comes to mind
Are those things set in rubber in a country lane
In an effort to Indicate the white line
On the darkest of nights so I'll do my best to explain
How a very bright individual set his mind to work
And pondered how the situation he could improve
To make motorists aware of their position in the road at
night
And enable them to drive a course so smooth
Then driving home one night his headlight beam caught a
cat
Walking towards him and it's eyes lit up like beacons
ahead
Just think what might have happened if the cat had
walked the other way
Then he may have invented a pencil sharpener instead

Dennis Shrubshall   2nd September 2011

Comparisons

I can see you there on the Verandah
Catching up with the latest news
Too see how things are in Sydney or Perth
Or merely watching the Kangaroos
It must seem all so different
From when you were in the U K
With a 9 - 5 job in the City
And commuting to work each day
But me every morning I rise at dawn
After Brekkers think what shall I do
Shall I out with the brushes, do some painting
Or hang just a door or two
Maybe I'll get my trusty trowel out
Then lay a few hundred bricks
And build someone a nice new garden wall
And hope to be finished by six
Then away with the tools, and off home I go
And after a rest perhaps I'll have time
To sit at the faithful computer
And write a few more words in rhyme

Dennis Shrubshall   21stst July 2007

201

Birds

In the Winter, trees are bare
Robins we can easily see
Frost is always in the air
The Redbreasts hopping from tree to tree
Ever vigilant they move about
Moving from grass to branch
Hoping someone's thrown out food
Their hunger perhaps to staunch
To find some food it is a must
For our little feathered friends
Unwanted crumbs, perhaps a crust
They're glad when Winter Ends.
In the tree there hangs a stand
To fill with scraps finds and such
For the constant flow of little Birds
Who need the food so much
The delicacy they all appreciate
Blue Tit, Sparrow and Wren
I've watched through the window, as they sit and wait
For a refill of nuts once again.
They've eaten their trill
As I watch ever hopeful that I
In this cold Season, for whatever reason
A Greenfinch might identify.
Snow in the trees and thick on the ground
And the food although already sparse
Was impossible to be found.

From nowhere's appeared a half loaf of Bread
Round which Starlings are beginning to prance
Small birds in the branches start avalanches
In their eagerness to be fed
Spring's come with a rush
And there's a Hen Thrush
Selecting a site for her nest
Where day after day, on her eggs she will lay
Making sure none she will crush.
They hatch from their shells, this hungry brood
Ever waiting for Mother supplying their food
But as they have grown and their wings start to sprout
They've kicked their hard-working Mother out.
Summer now and the Larks all sing
Warmth the Summer birds will bring
House Martins arriving with the Swallow
In mud and puddle she loves to wallow
With mud she fills her beak and leaves
To build her nest beneath the eaves, of the nearest House
from which she'll dive
For food to keep her chicks alive
Always in anticipation
They'll fly with her to Winter migration.

Dennis Shrubshall

First Love

Can you sit in the chair and just ponder
When the first love of your life you met
It is probably something you cherish
A memory you'll never forget
When you met as the park gates were closing
And the Sunset was there in the West
Then you walked hand in hand
In your own Wonderland
Was your new boyfriend really impressed
Did the perfume you were using affect him
Was it maybe Chanelle No. 5
And was he a real snappy dresser
Or perhaps about to contrive
The reason he liked your acquaintance
Your hair and the way that you dressed
Was it your smile and personality
Were they the things that he liked the best
Your next date was likely the Cinema
With two seats in the rear stalls
Only to find the Film breaking down
And the whole place was full of Catcalls
But you'd both spent the evening together
Young love in it's first bloom
And at home was it bliss
When you shared your first kiss
As Mum & Dad left the room
But those days are now far behind you

As you sit alone in your chair
Was that first love your one and only beau
Or the start of a lifelong affair
So now as you look to the mirror
Have your Blonde locks turned Silver or grey
Do you walk with a stoop, do your shoulders droop
Or are you striding upright each day
Is that first love still there beside you
A lifelong romance in every way

Dennis Shrubshall   22nd August 2007

Grandparents

A thought just came across mind
On how the times have changed
Relating to Nan's and Grandad's
And how their roles are now rearranged
When I was but a youngster
My Father's parent's had passed away
So I only had one Nan & Grandad
But I thinks it's fair to say
That every growing child needs them
In their early and formative years
For often they're the ones to make you laugh
Or be present to help you dry your tears
For me my Grandad was a stern man
With waxed moustache and a goatee beard
He'd let you help with jobs in the garden
Clean the rabbits and see the chicken run cleared
And Gran was a little old lady, with hairy chin
And her hair measured in length was 3 feet
Which was plaited into 2 plaits daily
And then tied in bun to keep it neat
With long hairpins that looked like stillettos
Which she rammed in with perfect aim
And dressed in a gown that went down to the floor
But wore button up boots just the same
And at that time Aunts and Granny's expected a kiss
Placed on their cheeks although it was plain
That most children never looked forward to this

By the look on their face of distain
But Nan & Grandad had the magic of love
Making sure to give them treats
Maybe a little personal gift
But most times a big bag of sweet
Time passes by with the wind of change
Grandparents roles are different by far
Instead of arriving on a twopenny bus ride
The children turn up by car
They teach Nan & Grandad the world of technology
For some it is hard to understand
That the youngsters want them to use a Computer and
Internet
Perhaps a chat online is what they have planned
The Girls want Nan to take them shopping to buy goodies
Or maybe take them for a visit to the Zoo
Where the boys look to Grandad to join them in a bike ride
And take them to the park to play football too
For Xmas now the scheme has altered
No longer Dolls and Chocolate and a mechanical Toy
But Computers , Bikes and Mobile phones
Is the method they now employ
No longer do they play Monopoly or Scrabble
"I spy" or perhaps a game of chess
But prefer to sit and watch the T V
To see why the world's in a mess
And sometimes the Grandparents are far from their minds
Out of sight out of sound some might think
But they always know who to come to
If they need money or food and drink
So now that I've brought the subject to mind
In front of your eyes to read
Is there something that applies to you or your Family
Maybe a lesson there to heed
With Christmas just round the corner
There's something I'd ask youngsters to do
Get on the phone at this very moment
A nd say " Hi Nan   Hi Grandad how are you

Dennis Shrubshall   3rd December 2011

Highland Home

Ahm nae the man ah used to be
And I cannae walk this way again
To see the wee Scots Lassie
Who helped to ease ma pain
For I fought ma fight when the Pipes they blew
The sounds o the bonnie Heelands
That's what helped me through
The battle fields and horrors of war
The Rifles, Bayonets , Tanks and Guns
Casualties and Corpses by the score
But for masen the War was over
Tho' the Memory will never die
And even now after all these years
Each day ah sit wie a tear in ma eye
And ah think wie pride in ma Scottish Regiment
Long since disappeared from view
But still ah can hear the scurl o the Pipes
As though the Lads'll come marching through
Now for me ma legs are old
And ma former strength ah lack
In my heart ah ken ah cannae make it
But ah ken theers no way o going back
So ah'll walk my way thro' the heather
Whilst ah still can
In the lasting memory of a much younger man
Perhaps ah'll see the bonnie Lassie once more
In those Scottish hills that ah know best

And maybe share a dram or two
Then one day ah'll come tae rest
For it's here that ah was born & bred
It's here ah know that ah want tae be
As ah return to the Heelands the land o the brave
And stay there in Eternity

Dennis Shrubshall   19th July 2009

Israel

I've sat and thought so many times
Of the Jewish people's plight
For many their lives are spent at war
Even the Ladies are expected to fight
Alongside their gallant brothers in arms
In constant anticipation
Of yet another threat from their enemy
Trying to decimate the Jewish Nation
They all dream of Israel their homeland
Although many come from across the Sea
To be a part of the national heritage
And live their lives in humility
But so many find when they get to their homeland
That a battle may suddenly ensue
From other outside Religious extremists
Who never seem to think things through
When reading back in History of the Middle East
2000 years or more
It seems to me that the Jewish Nation
Have had predators at their door
Ever intent to deprive these proud people
Of a land they could call their own
And over the many years between
Hostility seems to have grown
Many have settled around the world
Successful in their chosen clime
But in Russia and Poland and Europe

They had to move on time after time
But when they settled in the U K or the U S of A
Ordinary balanced lives they could choose
Without fear of war or retaliation
No worry that their homes they would lose
But still today, as in times gone by
Jewish youth is eager to discover and find
The reason why their ancestors both past and present
Chose to leave their Heritage and Homeland behind
So still to this day they choose to return to Israel
To learn of their people's present day plight
Even join the Armed Forces as conscripts
To help to preserve Israel's right
To live in the land of their Fathers
In the hope that one day Hostilities will cease
And the Jewish Nation can live normal lives once again
In their Homeland in Happiness and Peace.

Dennis Shrubshall   23rd July 2011

Karen the Girl with a curl

One day many years ago
Oh ! so long ago it seems
I met my first female Hairdresser
The answer to any man's dreams
As I sat in the chair for the very first time
All nervous and very shy
'Cos I'd never had my hair cut by a Lady
But I just had to give it a try
As all the old Barbers had popped their clogs
Or decided on retirement
And then on to the scene came **Karen** from **Hairworks**
Sometimes I think heaven sent
And over the years there are Memories
And I can recall just some
Like when I met Karen's brother
And when she introduced me to her dear Mum
I remember too when the boys were born
And Jordan's a man himself now
And then along came Luka after a while
But Karen still managed to work somehow
And I know if anyone asked why she stayed
In Benfleet as Haidresser to us
She'd say my Salon is Happiness
And my customers cause no fuss
I know that some times she battled to work
Although truly under the weather
But her strong determination to beat her ailment

Managed to pull her together
So that once again she's behind the chair
With a Welcome Banner unfurled
Do you want aTrim a Perm or an Affro
Or do you want your hair Straightened or Curled
I know she'll think I'm cheeky for writing these lines
And probably hand me a big Red Card
But it's always nice to be in her company
Says " Shrubby the Essex Bard "

Dennis Shrubshall   9th April 2009

The Soldier and P T S D

For many a lad when leaving School
A question that Career Teachers would often pose
How are you going to spend your life
And surprising how many the Army chose
As their way to fulfil their yearning
To rid themselves of inhibitions and such
Whilst a useful Trade they were learning
A Soldier is not just a fighting man
Carrying a Rifle and living on his wits
But a highly trained Professional Man
Allocated to a Trade that he fits
He'll wear his Uniform proudly now
For promotion he is ultra keen
As he signs the form for 22 years
In the Service of the Flag, the Country and the Queen
He's ready to serve wherever he's sent
His personal life he may have to put to one side
Although many Soldiers are married men
To their wives there are matters they can't confide
One such Soldier I've had the pleasure to meet
And I've learnt a little of his Army life
Of the trials , torments and battles of War
And the affect it has had on Sue, his Wife
He's had his share of troubles and more
What I know of Peter is as a peace-loving man
But a tough Sergeant Major and ever keen
And while serving for a while in Oman

Much Death and destruction he'd seen
'tho the Theatre of War that he can't forget
That lives evermore in Peter's mind
Is the liberation of the Falkland Islands
Where he left many of his colleagues behind
The tragic events that befell the RFA Sir Galahad
The horror of a burning ship at sea, with death and
destruction all around
'til help arrived by Royal Naval Helicopter
To help stricken colleagues in trouble they'd found
They were side by side in this flying machine
As they flew to safety on another ship not far away
These were some victims of this savage war
And they'd witnessed carnage there that day
Simon Weston now renowned for the injuries sustained
Was but one with whom Peter was saved
'tho in this action he received 49% burns
Like true British Soldiers they all behaved
He served tours of duty in Northern Ireland
And many stories I am sure he could tell
Of the shootings, bombings and violence
That made Ulster a Military Man's hell
He'd served the Country and Regiment well
For many years until 1993
After all the years of Mental Stress
Medically Retired was he
Sue asks "where is the laughter, the" oomph" and the joy
From the lovely man Peter I wed
As she tries her best to comfort him
As tho'a lttle boy lost crying by his bed
At a Barbeque he suffered a panic attack
With the smell of the meat on the grill
Brought memories back from the Falklands again
Of the scene of the ship on fire, in his mind still
But for some like Peter Southern
No physical scars did they bear
But the psychological damage they sustained
Was horrendous beyond compare
For some the end of their Service Career
But fortunately others were able to carry on
Though sadly most of them totally unaware
That the nightmare would never be gone
They'd relive the events of that day many times

Re-awakening their Service Life's worst fears
At home alongside their loved ones
And they were now reduced to tears
For sadly in a Soldiers training
At no time are they ever taught
How to handle a situation like this
When they are left in life distraught
To the world outside Peter had remained unchanged
But his Wife Sue and Daughter both knew
The demons he fought , the nightmares, the Traumas
That this proud ex Soldier was going through
But as one they fought this together
To re-kindle the life they once knew
And on the Internet found out about "Combat Stress"
Then enquired what next they should do
He was referred to Audley Court ,in Shropshire, for a twice yearly stay
Amongst Military colleagues affected the same
So each is aware of the torments they all suffer
And it's there perhaps their lives they'll reclaim
The results when he returns are quite positive
They all wonder what the future has in store
Hoping that Peter will finally recover his lost life
And they can live as a Happy Family once more

Dennis Shrubshall   29th January 2009

Ponderance

I think it's always nice
To spend a few moments of one's time
To come on exMilitarymates
And read or write some words in rhyme
The subject really doesn't matter
'Cos it's just a bit of fun
And helps to raise a smile or two
Bring happiness to someone
Who otherwise may sit and wonder
What a miserable place in which we live
It's only just some words in rhyme
And not a lot to give
Perhaps to somebody less fortunate
Who has to live alone or even in care
Whose wants and needs are minimal
But has love and compassion to share
For motivation is a must in life
In good health or even poor
And nice to welcome a smiling face
As you open your front door
So whilst you write your words next
Think of peace and tranquility
And the lives of the less fortunate
Instead of thee goes he.

Dennis Shrubshall   10th September 2007

Ron's Rally

Hi Ron you rallied to the call
To post your thoughts in here
It's plain for one and all to see
You hold Rhymes Of The Cuff dear
Something you started so long ago
With such a humble beginning
For Members to add their words in Rhyme
Without their praises singing
Allan a long time contributor
Joins you when he can
To add words of wisdom or laughter
Like any ex-Serviceman
Or Woman too as it happens
Who likes to see the thread work right
And the person in mind is Sheila O
Ex-Wren from the Isle of Wight
But I'm a relative new boy
Learning the rules and state of play
And always scan these Hallowed Halls
To see if anyone's posted that day
Since first I posted some years ago
15,000 viewings did I find
And now with 33,000 in total
It indicates how pleasure is defined
For every word and every line
In Odes and Poems I write for pleasure
I hope that it gives to others, less fortunate

Perhaps motivation in their times of leisure
To read and maybe meditate
On times and occasions passed
To prove that even with ageing years
Sad and Happy Memories still last
So now as I finish this Sermon, Ron
May I utter these words, sincere
In the hope that others with lyrical words
Will come and join us all here .

Dennis Shrubshall   27th June 2009

The Sniper

Out on patrol in the cold night air
Our adversaries we're hoping to find
Ever alert and with utmost care
Travelling through an area that might be mined
To them the value of Life comes cheap
Cunning and ruthless the enemy of which we speak
Booby traps and snipers in concealment
Death and destruction the goal they seek
Under the guise of religion
The Terrorists all ply their trade
To kill and injure without compassion
As they wage their so-called Crusade
Because of all the deadly obstructions
Our progress is Oh! so slow
For each of us is fully aware
That most of our movements they know
Then all of sudden the crack of a shot
And a very small giveaway spark
Of a single snipers rifle
Which gives us a target in the dark
A decision is made to take the assailant out
Or maybe capture for interrogation
All weapons aimed at the target now
To return fire and settle the altercation
Sporadic fire from the distance
In answer to our fight back in the dark
And then a prolonged silence

Perhaps our ammunition had found it's mark
But now came the dangerous part
As we needed to assure our enemy was dead
For one false move by any of our crew
May mean we become the casualties instead
So stealthily we approached the building
Which had housed our deadly foe
Then we tossed a couple of grenades through the window
No compassion could we show
And once the dust had settled
Then we were able to see within
There lay the bodies of four young mercenaries
For terrorism had been their final sin
So once again we covered the ground
As we returned to our base once more
Each of us thankful of a successful night
In this terrible theatre of War

Dennis Shrubshall   28th November 2009

The Summer Rain

Now April's here has Winter passed
Will we see the weather change
From the cold grey skies and windy chill
To travel through Natures climate range
Torrential rain on the window cill
Snow showers perhaps hail and sleet
These are all the conditions that make
An English Winter complete
But now it's time to look to the future
To see what the Summer may bring
To follow in the path of warmer days
That we've witnessed with the onset of Spring
Broken now then by the occasional shower
Or late Frost in the early morning too
Which might affect the growth of early plants
Although they welcome the morning dew
And now as a May dawn is breaking
With a clear blue sky overhead
Then a hint of Sun that's rising in the East
But dampness underfoot as you tread
The well worn path around the garden
To see how the plants have progressed
As you pause by the newly planted Arbour
Do the Roses pass the fragrance test
So you're now in a dearth of Summer Sunshine
All the plants are growing really well
Now is when they need lots of moisture

And when they're in need it's so easy to tell
But the clear sky has started breaking up now
Heavy rain clouds start to form
Intermittent thunder and lightning
Pre-empting another Summer storm
So it's time to return indoors now
And maybe stare through the window pane
Maybe listen to the melodic pitter patter
And you'll hear the rhythm of the Summer Rain

Dennis Shrubshall   11th April 2009

Twilight

As the sun begins to fade
And the night is drawing nigh
Out of the window I set my gaze
To the slowly darkening sky
Which now has changed to a darkening Pink
That's edged with a ribbon of gold
It's a truly magnificent Sunset
A pleasure to behold
But as the day just slips away
The silence seems quite muted
Devoid of the myriads of birds
And songs liberally distributed
Amongst the hedgerows and the trees
Their joy was shown with singing
As freely they flew in their world in the sky
Or on some of the treetops clinging
Tho' now not a sign of a bird can be found
As the darkness of night closes in
Nocturnal animals on the ground
Their night-time scavenge to begin
I nearly forgot the wily old Barn Owl
Perched in the rafters since the morn'
Patiently awaiting the return of the fieldmice
On the floor, and eating the corn
Circling the chicken coops again
Was the fox on his nightly habit
Unless on his journey he might waylay

A poor unsuspecting rabbit
After these few hours of darkness
Whilst most of the people sleep
The sky is getting lighter, it seems
As the watch of the dawn we keep
And if we care to stand and listen
If only for a minute
Perhaps we'll hear the chorus of dawn
The Blackbird, The Lark and The Linnet

Dennis Shrubshall   19th January 2007

Victims of Combat Stress

I've thought long and hard of the mind of a soldier
Returning from a theatre of war
No physical scars visible to the naked eye
But he's not the young man he was before
The battles they fought they were many
Their colleagues they witnessed them die
Tho' in their hearts they felt the emotion
But they would have never been seen to cry
The noise , the horror, the smell of cordite
The dreadful sound of a passing shell
The scream of a colleague detonating a mine
They were sights and sounds they knew too well
But for them now the war was over
These terrible memories they alone had to keep
Buried there deep within their souls
But coming to life as they tried to sleep
For it's hard to explain that you are wounded
When no physical scars ever show
For they are the type that will heal , given time
But mental scars are too deep for others to know
Sympathy is ever at their doorstep
But understanding is their greatest need
To rid them of the demons deeply hidden within
And help them once again to succeed
To return to the life that they knew before
And live the life of an ordinary man
Although they are classed as War Veterans now

They were lads in their twenties when the battles began
So as they try to pick up the threads of their lives
To purge the memories and horror from their soul
For if it is left ignored and untreated
It may eventually take it's dreadful toll
So if you should meet one of these victims of combat
And I personally have met one or two
Shake their hands and discretely look deeply into their eyes
And see if their injuries are visible to you

Dennis Shrubshall   14th February 2010

When tomorrow comes

When starting out on the Road of Life
The rules are not hard and fast
But usually rely on the guidance of others
That have made mistakes in the past
Each chosen step you tread
May have some imperfection
Which then may indicate erroneously
To lead you in the wrong direction
When sometimes you come to a crossroads
And ponder to turn left or right
At times like these you have to choose
And hope the decision you make is quite
Correct for the path you wish to travel
And take each step with caution and care
Tho' no-one knows what tomorrow may bring
For happiness or sorrow may be there
So perhaps it's folly to plan too far ahead
But try to live one day at a time
As every day and hour that passes, we get older
And will never return to our prime
So it's never bad to ask advice
At the times when you are in doubt
For troubles shared are worries halved
And may be easily sorted out
For no Man, or Woman, is an Island
As on friendships most of us rely
To carry on our lives from day to day

As the hands of time go rushing by
So never dwell on the sadness of life
But look for the cloud with the Silver Lining
Followed by a cloudless blue sky
Where the Sun is endlessly shining
So rid yourself of a lonesome past
And open your heart to a friend
And share the joys that each day brings
For your solitude to end
As you pass this way but once they say
So enjoy every passing hour to extreme
Perpetuate your life with joy
Fulfill your wildest dream
And only then will you know the happiness
That love and friendship may enhance
To re-awaken your yesterdays
And give your new future a chance.

Dennis Shrubshall   22nd May 2009

Wootton Bassett

For many years in Wiltshire
A Military heritage lies
Training establishments for troops galore
RAF sites for the lads from the skies
But the past is dwarfed by the present
Where Brize Norton was top priority
Now RAF Lyneham is the destination
For the planes to land with solemnity
For it is here they return with the Coffins
Of fallen comrades and victims of war
As they land to the sound of a lone Bugler
How long will the Aircrews have this chore
With the Standards lowered as into the hearse
These proud warriors are placed with great care
And are covered with the Union Flag of Great Britain
Witnessed by so many Families gathered on the Tarmac
there
Now the cortege moves off on it's final journey
To bring these young Hero's home once more
To say goodbye to their friends and Families
For they perished on some far away foreign shore
And now as they approach Wootton Bassett
There is heard the sound of St.Bartholomew's Church Bell
Which alerts all the Town's population
Of the sombre occasion they now know so well
The crowds line the streets standing shoulder to shoulder
An as one all local business daily work stops

230

Some adults stand with children and Clerks leave their desks
And shopkeepers temporarily close their shops
Pensioners too are there in abundance
Many of them have seen Military life too
And always in attendance The Royal British Legion
To honour victims of combat passing through
All this in perfect silence to see the cortege pass
With heads bowed in this moment of reverence
Even from the lads from the pub have forsaken their glass
As the vehicles approach the Memorial the Legion order is given
For ex-Service Members and those Serving to salute
And 60 seconds later "down" is the order
To these comrades they've paid their last tribute
By some folk it is thought that Wootton Bassett compares to Arlington
With no rigmarole nor flowers or fuss
And you might have heard someone in the crowd mutter
There but for the Grace of God it could be one of us
And as the cortege makes it's way and disappears in the distance
Once more Wootton Bassett goes about it's business once again
Having reflected the thoughts of the Nation, in Remembrance
Their dedication and resolution will remain
The Mayor has said that this is a Town that shows it's respect
And we honour the return of the fallen as only we can
Perhaps in the hope that in the very near future
The end of these conflicts will be the plan
And one young lad had said with a tear in his eye
Of the sad occasion that he had witnessed here on this day
That Soldier who died was only 4 years older than me
And that sentiment many others would display
The tradition of the Town they say may have started years ago
When an Army Cadet on a paper mache' Senotaph laid
A Wreath , and started a competition for something more permanent

And with£30,000 a new Memorial in Bronze was built
within a decade
On these occasions there are rules for the British Legion
No Standards are flown but Berets may be worn on the
head
Medals and Decorations are discretely out of sight
As to attention they stand and look straight ahead
Someone has suggested " An Avenue of Heroes"
But rejected by the local population
Without change what we do is as a mark of respect
To Victims of Combat on behalf of the Nation
In 2 years from now RAF Lyneham is to close
And these scenes Wootton Bassett may witness no more
The once more RAF Brize Norton will be the destination
For troops returning from a foreign shore
But long before that time there is a fervent hope
That these sad repatriations will cease
With the cessation of Military involvement
And perhaps an everlasting Peace
As a Nation we owe our thanks to Wootton Bassett
And may they get the recognition they've truly earned
For in War there are never any winners
Nor seldom knowledge gained or lessons learned

Dennis Shrubshall   18th September 2009

Victim of Alzheimer's

Your plight is recognised Oh! so well
But Children do not fret
For she is still there, the Mum you knew
So do not get upset
She may not comprehend what you say
In another world she may live
But all the love she gave to you
Is still there for you to give
For as we reach the twilight years
For some it's not too kind
As all the lovely Memories
Become muddled in your mind
But patience is still a virtue
Even tho' at times a strain
Always ever hoping that things will come right again
The sympathy of others
Tho' little comfort or consolation
Is all that they can offer
As outsiders in the situation
I know from my experience
The tasks you have to face
To cover Oh! so many things
In such a little space
Of time which is always well filled
Multi tasking you do best
Which makes you so strong willed
And fit to face the test

So close your eyes and think awhile
Of the times and memories passed
And you'll realise why you must go on
For life is going so fast
And I'm sure in my heart as I have trodden
The road that you tread now
You'll find that super hidden strength
And you'll cope some how
For a Mum is something precious
As everyone will know
Whatever it takes you'll do it
And never let the Memories go.

Dennis Shrubshall   15th August 2008

Un-requited Love

Why do you sit and search your soul
Recalling events that have passed
When you lived each day without a care
How long would your happiness last
The future was there on the horizon
The world was your oyster it would seem
Then a special someone entered your life
Could this be the answer to your dream
Each single day a joy to behold
To enjoy each day as it came
Forgetting events that had now passed
Your life may never be the same
Could you really live on love alone
You were willing to give it a try
For each time this person entered your thoughts
It brought a twinkle to your eye
You walked life's path with a spring in your step
Romance in your heart every day
And really believing this would last forever
Would your life always stay this way
But then as so often happens
The light of love seemed to grow dim
Was the flame of your friendship about to extinguish
Could it be the fault of you or him
Trying to analyse where loves ardour had cooled
Where was the weak link in love's chain
Could you rekindle the flames of passion

Knowing your hopes may be dashed again
For life's road is littered with hearts that are broken
Until they are picked up again to mend
By someone who understands the pain and the torment
Who may eventually become your lifelong partner & friend
As you walk off into the Sunset
Hand in hand as you watch the Sun descend
Ever hopeful of a life spent together in love
It's the way most love stories end

Dennis Shrunbshall   19th June 2010

The Firm's Christmas Party

Now once again the time has come
The Season of Good Cheer
And the mandatory Office Party
With Food and Wine and Beer
So now I'm out of the shower
I've got to look my best
When I join all my fellow workers
For this year's Xmas Fest
I've telephoned for a Taxi
To save dear Hubby the chore
Of taking me to my night out
Like he's done so many times before
So by the time that I arrived at the Restaurant
The party was in full swing
All the girls were dancing
And the men the usual thing
Knocking back pint after pint
Instead of drinking in moderation
By the way they seem to be chucking them down
It's like they're drinking for the Nation
But us Ladies we are more in control
At the moment anyway
But what might happen later
It's very hard to say
The beer and wine is flowing nicely
And underneath the Mistletoe the girls are getting kissed
But some of the men hands are wandering

And some girls tell them to desist
But as we all know it is inevitable that someone goes over the top
Out of his brains, carries on until he's told to stop
But generally everyone's enjoying themselves
As most of them know the score
Sing up drink up and be merry my lads
Cos that's what the Party's for
And as the evening comes to a close
The Management call out loud and clear
I trust you've all enjoyed yourselves
Merry Christmas and see you all next Year .

Dennis Shrubshall   7th December 2009.

Streets of London.

When walking along the roads in London
There is so much to be seen
For Tourists visit from all over the World
Perchance they may see our Queen
In residence maybe at Buckingham Palace
Or perhaps view the Changing of the Guard
For if you are trying to fill your day
It really isn't very hard
You may wish to visit Museums
To see the gory sights the Waxworks affords
Or see the Royal Horse Guards as they parade
In Regimental Uniform embracing swords
But if you had moved away to the East End
Away from the City's bright lights
You may have witnessed what may have been a spoof
But it was one of the strangest sights
For there in the heart of Shoreditch
To the tones of a single Church Bell
There happened a bizarre yet comic event
Or that is the way I heard folks tell
For the bell that tolled was for a Funeral in the Church
And outside the Undertakers had parked their Hearse
When along came a recovery to remove the vehicle
And lifted it aboard to the sound of a curse
Then as this had happened the pall-bearers returned
Carrying their precious heavy load
All they could see to their amazement

Was their Hearse disappearing down the road
Now whether this be true or maybe a jest
I think you would agree with me
Anyone walking the streets of London
A   more   un-believable sight would seldom see

Dennis Shrubshall   5th March 2010

Peacekeepers

From the day we landed on Foreign soil
We knew not what to expect
Nor the reason for our presence there
But now in retrospect
Would it really have made any difference
As a Military Force we have a role to fulfil
To put into practice the skills that we've learnt
Hoping that we'd not have to kill
For that is the ultimate deterrent
When all normal reasoning has failed
And it's then you fight fire with fire
When your enemy may die by the bullet or on a bayonet
impaled
But a Soldier is a Professional man
And during his Service is never in doubt
When facing the enemy on the front line of attack
That a stray bullet may also snuff his life out
To be ever alert is a must in Combat
In order, perhaps to survive
And be part of a well formed Tactical Unit
So they all have chance to come out alive
Teamwork is imperative from beginning to end
Discipline is paramount too
For in a life threatening situation
The principal player may be you
And when the main battles are over
And it's hoped normality will slowly return

As a Soldier you still have a role to achieve
To help the offended Nationals to learn
Once more to create a Democratic State
Where the Pen is perhaps mightier than the sword
Free from rebellion or coups d'etat
And independence would be their reward
Then our Peacekeeping Troops may return home once
again
To U K's pleasant pastures green
Ever hopeful to carry on their life here at home
And also that the last of Warfare's horrors they'd seen
With a fervent hope that with Battle done
Was it all really worth the human cost
As the Lads with their heads bowed in a reverent silence
In Memory of the colleagues whose lives were lost.

Dennis Shrubshall   16th July 2009

242

What is Friendship

Friendship is not a commodity
But something to be earned
As I travel through my life
It's something that I've learned
It's Oh! too easy to scoff or laugh
Or take a name in vain
But amity is so important
And that's why I'll now explain
When you meet someone for the first time
A certain impression they'll make
Then it's up to you to follow it up
And decide which avenue you'll take
If you've both got off to a really good start
And each on the other depends
You'll each work hard to achieve your goal
And eventually become in-separable friends

Dennis Shrubshall   26th November 2010

Heroes all

Above us the drone of a plane in the sky
Making it's approach to land
Watched by many anxious people
As below on the Tarmac they stand
And as the huge aircraft comes to a halt
And their mighty engines to silence fell
There was an air of reverence and silence in the crowd
And expectance of sorrow and sadness as well
Once more the sight of pall bearers in Uniform
Board the aircraft to perform their solemn task
Accompanied by the sound of a solitary Bugler
At the return of fallen heroes, and again many may ask
How many more young Soldiers must perish
To free Nations where they are oppressed
But sadly return home as the victims of Combat
And here in England's Green Pastures will rest
Now down the ramp come the pall bearers
With National Flag draped coffin, looking terse
And march slowly across the Tarmac, with precision
To again fill a waiting hearse
One can feel sadness and regret in the air all around
And then as the final pall bearers have passed
They seemed to close their eyes in prayer
In the fervent hope that this occasion may be the last
With heads bowed as the large cortege starts it's
procession
To transport these Heroes on their last journey home

In the knowledge that they served in a fight against oppression
So that others in Foreign lands in Peace they may roam
For it is known that in War there is but one winner
And the Grim Reaper is his name
For the cost of War is not Financial that matters
But the huge loss of young lives is the shame

Dennis Shrubshall   16th October 2009

Yesterday's gone

I woke up this morning
Thought what shall I do
I'll forget all my past life
And start something new
I was really fed up
With the life that I led
So today I'll try fields anew
When I get out of bed
For a start I shall sort out
What's wrong with my life
And get rid of the troubles
Along with   sorrow and strife
In the past for the grief
There were always floods of tears
But now I shall look forward
To my happier years
Away with the handkerchief
For no tears will I shed
But daily I shall replace them
With laughter instead
But some place I must find first
For the memories I cherish
Away from the sadness
Which I will gladly see perish
And then on with my new life
Where my dreams will excel
But that is in the future

Which no one can tell
So onwards ever onwards
I shan't know 'til I try
And say "Hello " to tomorrow
And kiss yesterday goodbye

Dennis Shrubshall   1st June 2009

Where is the Love

Where is the love that once you knew
As it blossomed in your youth
The moon shone clear
And the Sun beams were bright
But did this disguise the truth
About how life can really be
As on life's road you travel
Tho' it make take so many years
The answers to unravel
For as you start upon the road
In dreams you still believe
How the Handsome Prince may come along
No thought that he might deceive
'Cos in those Fairy Tales you read
They have a Happy Ending
But love between a young couple
May soon see a cloud descending
When you sat in the room and your eyes first met
Was your heart all a'flutter and miss a beat
Did you ever think for one moment
It would end in lies and deceit
Oh Yes there were times you could jump for joy
And think of the happy times ahead
But alas sometimes things will go wrong
So you're there in the doldrums instead
Good times you'll always remember
Like the time you held your first child

You probably wept like the baby yourself
Completely and utterly beguiled
Which gave you the strength in those early days
To discover what life has in store
And should misfortune overtake you
You'll quickly show it the door
For then it will be time to open your heart
And seek in pastures new
To find love and compassion that you seek
Which may last the rest of life through

Dennis Shrubshall   28th October 2007

The Poppy Fields

We know not what is in the wind
Cast by Mother Natures hand
Or borne by the birds as they soar through the sky
Never selective of where the seeds land
An onward progression that never stops
Germinating from seeds however sown
Ensuring that yearly the fields hold crops
To be harvested when fully grown
Whether it be wheat or barley or oats
Which variety it's shade of gold denotes
But other crops their colours vary
Some variegated at the head
Except for acres and acres across the horizon
Creating a beautiful carpet of Red
Gently they wave their heads in the breeze
As the Autumnal Season appears
'tis the Poppy with it's silken leaves so gentle
Adopted from Flanders fields for Oh! so many years
In memory of all the Soldiers that fell there and died
Each year Millions of Poppies will show
To make sure that the Sacrifice that they made
Ever present today as it was long ago
Tho' gone from this life they are ne'er far away
Remembered in Reverence with all heads bowed
They gave their tomorrow for our today
So that with Peace in our lives we are endowed.

Dennis Shrubshall   17th October 2009.

"Gizmo"

There's an old and ancient saying
That the Dog is the man's best friend
But that applies to a woman too
Although quite often to defend
Tho in the case I have in mind
Of facts I have but few
There's a certain lady I know
Whose Dog is her pet and friend too
They've been together now for a year or two
I don't honestly know quite how long
But every single day that passes
Means their friendship grows more & more strong
I imagine he was only a Puppy
When their 2 paths just crossed
But I know that the time they spend apart
Each of them is quite lost
For he's an English Springer crossed Border Collie
A really compatible blend
On the one hand a dog who loves herding sheep
And the other playful and fun loving to the end
A Collie loves to work and chase everything in sight
Without exercise he can really be a pest
But a Springer loves playing in puddles and mud
Which puts many owners to the test
Now when you put these two breeds together
An amazing creation you will find
An enthusiastic and affectionate companion

Is the best description that comes to mind
Now "Gizmo" is the name of the dog of whom I speak
And seems to know each word his owner's spoken
But the love that they share is immeasurable
Where time spent together's a mere token
He knows the time to wake and stand by the door
For a run round the garden and return
To sit by her owners side or maybe on her feet
And wonder what new tricks today he'll learn
In the middle of each day he'll stand by the door
As his owner walks up with leash in hand
It's time now for walks and games and paddling in the puddles
And it's not really hard for "Gizmo" to understand
Then when the walk is over and back home again
He'll lay around nor far from his owners feet
Quite happily dozing for a few moments
As he knows it won't be long before he'll eat
Till late in the evening once more he'll search the garden
Or maybe just a walk in the yard
Another day is finished for "Gizmo" and his Lady
And they say a working "Dog's Life" is hard

Dennis Shrubshall   10th February 2012

Forget me not

Although I'm no longer within your arms
For that ever welcome embrace
You'll feel my presence around you
In every mortal place
For me the suffering is over
No more will I feel the pain
But I know that sometime in the future
We'll both be together again
So think of me each and every day
As to the Heavens your eyes you cast
For the sorrow and loneliness you feel today
Will soon become a thing of the past
Remember a Soldier always has two loves
A caring Mother and a beautiful Wife
But because he fights for his Country
In Combat it may one day cost him his life
So weep not for me at my graveside
Where I know that my company you'll keep
And think of me now as I always was
Except that here I lie fast asleep
For I know nevermore in your arms will , I, you hold
Nor from you anymore feel a warm caress
But always remember the love that we had
And try all the tears to suppress
Look forward to a bright new tomorrow
With me just in another place
For I'll never forget the love of my life

Or the lovely radiant smile on your face
So think of me each and every day
And as you lay down on your pillow to sleep
I'll always be there to watch over you
As on my Heavenly watch I keep
So live happy and healthy from now my love
And may you a long life complete
Then may you never have to say goodbye, but adieu
Until finally again we may meet .

Dennis Shrubshall   20th September 2009

Falklands 30 years on

History is made in many forms
Not known to one and all
Some of the facts are documented
Others older persons recall
A conflict that is ever in my mind
Well past my Service time
When the biggest Armada since World War 2
Left the U K shores for the South Atlantic clime
To thwart the claim by Argentina
To seize a Sovereign Isle
That was the task of the British Military force
Carried out in their own inimitable style
But many men suffered and many men died
In the Falklands all those years ago
And many were mentally wounded
The scars of their wounds never show
For the damage to them was buried deep
In their souls and in their mind
With an ever constant reminder
Of the colleagues they left behind
The horror of battle the noise and the smell
For the survivors is with them yet
So let's bow our heads and remember them all
Our heroes we must never forget.
As we go about our everyday chores
How many would stand and think of the cost
Of that tragic conflict in the South Atlantic
Where all those young lives were lost.

Dennis Shrubshall   10th July 2011

Bottlenose Dolphins

Vast are the wonders beneath the seas
Where life in abundance abounds
Creatures and Fish   and Mammals
Each in their favourite hunting grounds
But we're now in the world of the Dolphin
An household favourite for some
A Sea Life attraction for many
And from across the world they come
To see these beautiful creatures
That swim the oceans deep
But some are cared for in Sea Life Centres
Where entertainment pays for their keep
In the wild Bottlenose Dolphins survive
In Oceans the whole world wide
And many are spotted from ships cruising
Watched with interest from the ship's side
They are Family orientated
And in "pods" together they'll swim
For safety from their predators
Or deterring the hunters whim
Although athletic and mobile in stature
Their sight is very poor
So they rely on an inbuilt sonar system
To search for food on the ocean's floor
As well as direction finding apparatus
When travelling areas anew
Perhaps in search for a mating ground

Essential for them and food too
For each Dolphin has a large daily appetite
Squid and fish they'll eat 30 pounds
Which they locate with their personal Sonar
By the various echoes and sounds
It takes 15 years to reach maturity
Tho' females are quicker it seems
A strong ritual of communication applies
Before reproductive schemes
The female will carry the calf for 12 months
Swimming with the "pod" by her side
And when the calf is finally born
Midwife Dolphins their skills are tried
As they swim side by side with the family
The new calf will be nursed for 6 years
Only then will it have to fend for itself
Unless a large predator appears
When all the Dolphin "pod" will fight as one
On their survival it often depends
These wonderful creatures of the sea
Known as the Ocean's best friends.

Dennis Shrubshall   7th December 2011

Curly - My LIfe

My story started long ago
On the banks of the Mediterranean Sea
In the City of Beirut in Lebanon
Which became a birthplace for me
My mother was a Nursing lady
The Red Cross organisation was the employer she had
Working in a local Hospital
And that's how she met my Dad
She was blessed with four loving children
There was Sister Josephine and me
Then Joseph and George were our 2 brothers
Making up our Happy Family
Technology was my Dad's first love
As an Aeronautical Engineer
Employed by Middle Eastern Airways
At Beirut Airport which was really quite near
His occupation meant a lot of study
And for some more knowledge to England he went
To me as a growing teenager
It seemed the journey was heaven sent
Then out of the blue our lives all changed
With the outbreak of a Lebanese War
And my parents were in a quandary
With 4 children to cater for
Then Dad was offered a new position
In New York City in the U S of A
Where he could work for the Airlines again

And we as children could live, learn and play
I was a mere 14 years old at the time
But with my sister and brothers we coped quite well
To cope with this huge transition in our lives
An event which no-one could foretell
We all adapted to our new life very easily
Being bi-lingual an advantage it would seem
As we settled into the local community
Not a nightmare but a beautiful dream
At 19 I met and married my Prince Charming
And Robert then gave me his name
Regardless of the age difference
Romance was the name of the game
Then suddenly like a bolt from the blue
Our Happiness came to a halt
Robert was diagnosed with Brain Cancer
Sadly nobody was really at fault
His life was saved by the Surgeons knife
And his personality suffered too
For after such a serious operation
He was no longer the man I knew
I was pregnant then with a baby son
Then another son and Twin boys too
The thought of a lovely Family
Might help to pull me through
The worrying years
The depression I suffered and shock to my life
Caring for a Family and Husband
And still a faithful and loving Wife
I had Noah & Justin and Elijah
But after a short life Daniel passed away
Tho the other three lads gave me all there love
To make up for the loss it's only fair to say
Then some time later whilst out in my car
I parked with tears in my eyes and distraught
When an Ambulance passed with siren and blue lights
Giving me cause for serious thought
It was then I registered for Medical School
And after my Graduation
Took up the role of a Paramedic
Which for 12 years was my occupation
The shifts I worked sometimes 16 hours
And did my important job well

The pressure of severe depression lessened
As though being released from a spell
But sadly now the man that I married
Year on year more remote Robert seems
Love and romance are a thing of the past
I'm alone to live with my dreams
But I'll never abandon the man that I married
Perhaps I'll meet a friend with love to share
As I look to the end of a Rainbow
Maybe find happiness once again there

Dennis Shrubshall   13th November 2011

Birds demise

Why did they have to shoot me
I so enjoyed my avian life
Flying high above the battlefields
Away from care and strife
I perched and ate the bird seed
And sang my little song
Flew like an angel in the sky
I was happy all day long
I perched there in the treetops
Even the washing line too
Tried not to foul the laundry
Like other naughty birds do
Now someone's gone and shot me
Bringing my life to an end
Which is sad because I spent my life
Trying to be everyone's friend
But that's the way the cookie crumbles
Enjoy life while you may
For as sure as the Sun rises tomorrow
They'll be joining me one day

Dennis Shrubshall   24th June 2010

An Officer not a Gentleman

Once upon a time many years ago
As her teens were coming to and end
And though they were times she would rather forget
She wanted to enjoy life rather than pretend
As her early life in a broken home
Perhaps denied of sympathy and care
Which most young ladies will take for granted
But for her the cupboard of love was bare
A pretty lass by any standard
Tho' shy and a trifle naïve
To know that she longed for male company
Is not too hard to believe
And then one time on an evening out
When she visited the local Fair
There was this tall and elegant Military Officer
And she could not avoid his stare
Was this her Knight in shining armour
Would her romance begin right there
For this young Lass had thoughts of a Military career
Which may have been uppermost on her mind
Could this Young Officer have the key to the door
Beyond which perhaps her future she'd find
They met and talked for hours it seemed
For there seemed Oh! so much to say
As he pledged his everlasting love
Then with sadness she turned and walked away
Whilst travelling home with a heavy heart
Came the tears as she started to weep

And threw herself on the bed, disconsolate
To eventually cry herself to sleep
Days later she realised the error she's made
And tried contact by telephone
Only to be told by a fellow Officer
That her Beau to War had now gone
As she replaced the phone with a heart that was broken
And once more the torrents of tears
But then wrote the love letters, and prayed for his return
For weeks and then months which turned to years
Then out of the Blue came a phone call
And it was the voice of another female who spoke
He's mine now so stay away, then he confirmed it
And it was then that the young Lassies heart broke
So deep was the hurt that she suffered that day
To herself she made a solemn vow
No more would there be a Special man in her life
She would live her life on her own now
Time and again the Young Officer tried to contact her
But his calls she would always reject
For the depth of the damage he'd imposed upon this damsel
On a young lady, herself unable to protect
The years then passed and she got on with her lonely life
As now a wise woman of the World was she
And she carried on her career in the City
For from her previous worries she now seemed free
'til one day whilst walking along on her own
Two men approached and placed a book in her hand
And told her to open it when she was home
Their reasons she would then understand
Then once she was alone in her bedroom
Turned the pages one at a time One then Two then Three
In front of her now was the photo of the Young Officer
Who treated her so dastardly
People may have said he never loved her at all
But just used her as a pawn in his cruel game
She remembered asking him for a Photo as a Memento
Until a dream   a dreadful nightmare he became
But now the book has raised a question in her mind
Do I still love him and does he still love me
When I asked the young lady how she knew all these facts
She said " I know because I am that young lady you see"

Dennis Shrubshall   5th November 2009

263

A Winter Walk

It's early morning in December
A chill wind fills the air
As we stroll through the countryside
Without worry or care
For this is the Ramblers paradise
As we stroll along side by side
And a Rabbit dashes for cover
From the predators to hide
And there in the hedgerow
A wily Fox we espy
Vanishing into the undergrowth
Whilst we're passing by
The sun has not yet risen
As we were out with the dawn
The time for Nature lovers
To see the best of the morn
The frost in the treetops
Like a silvery gown
And as the birds flutter in the trees
Causing particles to drift down
On the unsuspecting travellers
Who are walking below
Sometimes the fall is heavy
Giving a semblance of snow
There are horses in the field now
And may have been there for days
Searching the frosty landscape

For some fresh grass where they may graze
Although it's early on Sunday
Some folk still have a daily chore
To round up the Dairy herd
For the Milking shed once more
Then onward we walk now
In the early morning mist
Never knowing what we might see next
To add to an ever-growing list
Of the wonders of Nature
On which people write and talk
And today we're the lucky one's to see them
On our Sunday morning Winter Walk

Dennis Shrubshall   2nd January 2011

Alice

Some people believe in a Wonderland
In Fairy Tales it was Alice
Where all her dreams came true
And she finished up in her Palace
But life although is sometimes similar
With experience of sadness and joy
And plays a part in every life
Through the manner we may employ
But I have a friend named Alice
And have known her many years
We've shared many happy hours together
And I've been there to help her dry the tears
Unfortunately there was a man in her life
Who lied and would ever deceive
So she made up her mind to confront him
Perhaps her anger to relieve
With a growing anger inside her
She started to drink to ease the pain
Which prompted her to take action
After drinking to excess once again
And on this fateful evening
She took her daughter along for the ride
Tragedy occurred as her truck overturned
On the journey, and her dear daughter died
Now Alice has a dog and her Husband
If between them she was asked to choose
I'm not a gambling person

But I think the Hubby would lose
And after the sad event in her life
She turned to drink to ease the pain
Knowing her behaviour caused the accident to happen
And she'd not see her beloved daughter again
Her life is now spent in a home that's pristine
With nothing to seem out of place
A house that's always tidy and clean
But no longer a smile on her face
It's sad to think of my friend in her plight
A pal that I've long known as Alice
She'll never be free of that terrible night
Away from the world in her Palace.

Dennis Shrubshall   16th February 2011

Armistice Day

It's 11 am on Armistice Day
A truly reverent scene
Row upon row of yesterday's Soldiers
Veterans now but just as keen
As they answered the call as young men & Women
To fight for the right to be free
From the possible threat of Dictators
Stealing their country's liberty
Year after year since 1918
ex Servicemen young and old
Return here to the Cenotaph
To remember fallen colleagues bold
They march so proud, with their heads held high
Chair bound and invalids too
To honour the dead and fallen
Brothers in arms through and through
Every possible Service represented there
Thinking as one, in accord
There were those who saved their homeland
Those who fought terrorism abroad
With their heads to the right, as they pass the Queen
To give the time-honoured salute
Today they're here to pay homage
From the Veterans to the raw recruit
They've come to a halt and there's silence
For the Service and then the wreath's are laid
Then as their heads and standards are lowered

Each in his own way prayed
In unison with the lone Bugler
As he blew the Last Post
Many with a tear on their faces
Remembering their personal Ghost
Of battles past when colleagues they'd lost
Tho' never far from their mind
And on an occasion such as this
Comfort and peace they can find
The call now comes for " Attenshun"
The Bearers their Standards now raise
The Old Soldiers march off in formation
To conclude one of Britain's proudest Military Displays.

Dennis Shrubshall   9th November 2008

Artist on the Shore

I lay awake in the early morn
Waiting for the dawn to break
Would this herald a perfect start to the day
When a trip to the beach I take
Slowly I rise and get myself ready
The first signs of daybreak now show
As I pack my lunch and fill my flask
It will soon be time to go
Away on the distant horizon
The sky now a pale shade of Blue
As the night slips away in the distance
There's a small cloud here and there too
So it's time for me to start walking
With my easel and well used Palette in my hand
Board and Brushes and paint in my satchel
And hope the day goes as I planned
As I amble along the cliff top
Then down the cliff path I descend
To an isolated spot on a deserted beach
Idyllic beauty is there without end
So my sandals are in my bag now
 I slowly walk barefoot across the sand
And there up ahead is my subject today
As the seashore and cliffs my eyes have scanned
I' ve set up my easel and board now
The Sun rises higher in the Sky
Bringing to life Natures wonders

Before my discerning artistic eye
Pastel Blue for the Sky now upon the board
Broken here and there with Grey of the cloud
Darker Grey and White and Black for the Seagulls
As they swoop and dive their shrill cries ever loud
The Grey of the Cliffs interspersed with some Green
A pleasant contrast against the Golden sand
Then Green Blue and Grey as the tide is coming in
White froth on the Beach as the rolling waves land
Coloured dinghies bobbing up and down at anchor
And a Fishing Boat is heading out to sea
Propellors agitating water to White foam in it's wake
And I sometime's wish that Fisherman was me
On this isolated beach I am joined now
Two Sea Anglers arriving with their gear
And they set up for a morning's fishing
Chattering away but I'm too far off to hear
So it's out now with their Beach Caster rod and lines
And the chosen baits placed upon the hook
Then raise their rods and cast seawards together
In the hope that some Sea Fish they'll take home to cook
So now I included these two Anglers
As I continued to paint this image on the sand
But I think that my Artistic task will finish
Before some sizeable fish they land
So now as the basis of this scene is painted
And my footsteps up the path I retread
My Sachel on my shoulder, Easel Board & Palette too
I'll paint the final touches in the Studio instead

Dennis Shrubshall   7th January 2011

Deep in thought

I read your verse with thought so deep
And in my mind I try to keep
An image of a gentle soul
Who carries her maternal role
'Tho fate to her has been unkind
Yet still she carries on refined
To beat the demons lurking there
And even in moments of despair
Remembering loving moments past
Yet to the future her mind will cast
To Talents regained in Acrylic and oil
She carries on her daily toil
And thanks the lucky Stars above
To regain an un-requited Love

Dennis Shrubshall   2008

Horses

It is often said that a man's best friend
Is one of the Canine kind
But if you look back in your book of life
An even stronger friend you will find
Just think of a stroll in the country
Where into fields you would casually gaze
How many times did you catch sight of Horses
Trotting across the field to graze
And the extra pleasure in Springtime
When the Mares keep a watch over their foals
As they frolic about on their spindly legs
And their playfulness Mother controls
Do people remember the poor Pit Ponies
That spent their life underground in the dark
Maybe a Shetland or an Exmoor pony
Running wild in Dartmoor National Park
Then running on the Fells of Cumbria
Fell Ponies at home in rough terrain
And if you happen to visit the Forest in Hampshire
New Forest Ponies living wild once again
The Shetland Pony is a favourite with the children
A docile breed and a size so small
Compared to a full grown Shire Horse
A mere 10 hands the Shetland but the Shire is 17 hands
tall
The Suffolk is also a workhorse
Stand 16 hands or maybe a little more

Both of these horses full of power
Built to pull heavy loads for evermore
The Arab is a proud equestrian Animal
Bred mainly for competition and shows
And the Mustang he's a fiery breed they say
Bred to ride and their reputation everyone knows
And the last in the line is the thoroughbred
Born to have a Jockey on his back
And standing a full 16 hands high
Always happy when running round the track
The Shire and the Suffolk Punch on farms still may be
found
'tween the shafts of a trailer or shackled to a plough
But in the past were seen on Britain's streets pulling carts
For Delivery Men but they no longer do that now
At one time horses were a main source of transport
And their welfare always in their riders hearts
Some between the shafts of a stage coach
A Hansom Carriage or even single Dog Carts
But out on the prairies and ranches of America
Or the Wild West Townships that we only see upon the
silver screen
Where the horse is essential for rounding up the cattle
And quite a lot of Mustangs are seen
But return if you will to the present day
Where machinery has taken place of the Horse
They still have a function in the world today
Revered by their owners as always
Content to be in a stable with plenty of hay
They're still used by Police for patrol work
Controlling a demonstrative crowd
Groomed and fed by their riders
Doing a job of which they're both proud
Still used too by the British Army
In the Hussars to safeguard The Queen
Where they parade daily in front of visitors from across the
world
Who flock to view this Buckingham Palace scene
In the countryside Horses still go hunting
With their riders as they're hunting the wily Fox
Supported by the local Poultry farmers
To stop him ravaging their stocks
Still busy is the village Blacksmith

With his Furnace , bellows and shoeing tool
Final shaping on his trusty Anvil
To shoe the Horses of the village riding school
So if you hear the clatter of the hooves upon the
cobblestones
And you're in London you need not think too hard
Because you are soon about to witness the Parade
Of The Changing of the Guard

Dennis Shrubshall   16th January 2011

G'day sport

Now Australia is a land far far away
"down under!" to us in the U K
It's part of the Antipodes
Or so I've heard people say
In the southern Hemisphere
Though I'm not sure what they are
I only know you go by Sea or Fly
'cos you won't get there by car
Now the men might just say to you
G'day Sport howya doing today
Wudja like a tube of Foster's
To take your thirst away
And with a throat as dry as a "Dingo's donker"
" Thanks mate" is about all you can say
Now the "Sheila's" look alright to me
Especially when they smile
But if you tell them you're a "Pommie B"
They're like to run a mile
Occasionally you will see the Aborigine
And mostly doing menial tasks
Then when he's finished working
A couple of beers is all he asks
The Dingo's are in the "outback"
And Wallabies and Kangaroos
They don't respect the human race
And lead the life they choose
Now if you're sitting on the Verandah

Sipping an ice cold beer
There's pretty birds and Koala Bears
But they never venture too near
Now if it's nice & hot and you fancy a change
Get yourself down to Bondi Beach
Where lots of sun-tanned Ladies in Bikinis
Make sure they keep out of reach
So if you happen to be in Australia
Enjoy every day as best you can
And say "Hi Cobber" to the next person that passes in the Street
Cos it might be a bl!!!!dy Englishman

Dennis Shrubshall   8th September 2011

277

24 Months of a Lifetime

I wore the Queen's Uniform for 24 months
And not a single day more
As that was all that was required of me
To follow other conscripts before
I was not a Military man by choice
But the Law of the Land decreed
That each and every fit young man
Would fill Great Britain's need
For the maintenance of a Military Might
On Land and Sea and in the Air
To counter any threat of War or oppression
That might have been lurking here and there
Across the European Continent
And varied parts of Asia too
Where the services of the British Military Man
Was proven through and through
I never knew the smell of cordite
Or heard the scream of an enemy shell
But the lads in Korea, and Borneo and Malaya
They all knew these dangers so well
Where they fought on the hills of Korea
Against an enemy they were outnumbered
But in the swamps of Malaya as they waded after
Terrorists
In constant fear of leeches and disease they were
encumbered

But each and every one carried out the task that they were given
And they all wore their Uniform with pride
Even tho' it was not their chosen profession
They fought with Regular Soldiers by their side
But sadly as is always the case in conflict
On the Battlefield many young Military men are lost
In order to defeat the Oppressors and the Tyrants
The sacrifice of Soldiers lives a terrible cost
But only when the 2 years were over
Then this Country's young conscripts returned
And once again could follow their chosen career
With the knowledge of the Service Life they'd learned
But I don't think the average man on the street knew
What a debt the World at large owed
To the National Servicemen who were paid a mere pittance
And on whom Honours were seldom bestowed

Dennis Shrubshall   17th May 2009

Meerkats

Pets are very varied
In the wide world as a whole
Important to so many people
Is their domestic role
There are Cats & Dogs & Mice & Rats
Of every size and breed
All pets regarded by someone
If only for their hypnotactic eyes they need
But the animal that I have in mind
Neither canine or feline it be
But a member of the Mongoose family
Some wild but some in captivity
For the Meerkat has so many features
That appeal to those looking for a pet
They are tiny yet entertaining
But Live happily domesticated with no regret
In the wild they may live for ten years
If their Predators they can avoid
But five years longer as domestic pets
Where no threats or enemies are employed
The Meerkat's natural home is the Desert
Grouped in Gangs , or Clans or a Mob
Which may contain up to 50 Meerkats
Each one having it's own job
They like the soft sand to dig for food
Like worms , crickets and lizards or small snakes
But sometimes live on birds, eggs or fruit

Maybe Scorpions too if their fancy takes
They are born with hair but not full coats
Their eyes are closed and they cannot see
And their ears are closed too for the first 14 days
21 days underground for their own safety
And when they emerge from there underground home
The adults all stand around as tho on guard
Ready to protect the youngsters from Predators
As the Kalahari Desert living is hard
New Meerkat groups are formed by females who are
evicted
As passing male Meerkats they attract
Producing more families increasing their numbers
And their sentries making sure they stay intact
So if you fancy a pet that is different
Don't chose a Hamster or a Rat
Just pop down to the local pet shop
And purchase yourself a Meerkat.

Dennis Shrubshall   7th August 2012

Debra's Dilemna

I'm sitting alone and I'm thinking
What can I do in the coming weeks
I don't want to get bored doing nothing
After Harvesting my carrots and leeks
I've vacuumed the carpet and dusted the shelves
And I've had a chat on the phone to Mom
Tidied the Kitchen & finished reading the book
And I've written a letter to Tom
I've cleaned the floor and the cooker too
After making cookies and a cake
I've tidied the cupboards and cleaned the closets
And fished a few hours in the lake
My mind it seems to be in turmoil
There must be some things I can do
To get me away from this boredom
Before this day is finally through
I've found my Computer is broken
So I can't chat to friends on the Internet
But I used to manage somehow before
So why am I so upset
Then by way of a change when ready for bed
I moved the roll from one side to the other
And when I awoke in the morning
It took me a while to recover
I'm immediately thinking why's the roll over there
Instead of it's usual place
And then I looked in the mirror and saw

The bewildered look on my face
So I cast my mind back and remembered
The reason for the Roll's change I could see
And the person who did the dastardly task
Was actually none other than me
So having looked back at the things that have happened
I have an ultimate decision to make
Shall I repeat all the tasks that I did yesterday
Or shall I merely go fishing in the lake.

Amended by **Dennis Shrubshall**   31st July 2011

Sitting in the Garden

I was sitting in my Garden Room listening to the radio
Thinking of my life, so many years ago,
The things I did as a child, and as a Girl.
That now my body is racked with aches and pain,
I shall never be doing such things again.
I would meet my young friends in the park.
And play with them until it was dark.
The hardest thing we had to decide,
Was whether we would go backwards down the slide.
Oh yeah, there was one other thing.
How high we dare go on the swing?
Those childhood days went quickly past,
And I became grown up at last,
Exams passed, my school days were over,
I had not realised I'd been living in clover.
There was now less time to play.
I had to go out and earn my pay.
Now, I found that this was hard to do,
It seemed everyone was watching you,
To see if you would make the grade,
And put your workmates in the shade,
I came to realise that I must try,
To be the apple of my boss's eye.
This meant that I must do my best,
And to work much harder than the rest,
And by this means I would succeed,
In providing for my every need.
And now I'm old I can look back,
Thankful that there's nothing that I lack.

As I sit here I must face the truth,
And accept that I have lost my youth,
Thinking of the things I used to do.
 sitting here in my Garden room, listening to the radio.
Time to reflect on yesteryear
To think of days long gone
As you reclined in comfort in the garden
And for company had the Radio on
You thought of the days as a young girl
When you ran and skipped with ease
On the way for a meeting in the Park with your friends
To enjoy yourselves in any way you please
There were swings and even a roundabout
Which you could all jump on and ride
As you sit and contemplate what to do next
Perhaps come down backwards on the slide
Though childhood at the time passed so slowly, so it
seemed
But on reflection those days went so fast
And you realised your schooldays were over
When your final Exams you had passed
And now into a young lady you had grown
Perhaps with tears that mixed with laughter
It was time for you to earn a living on your own
To succeed in life you have to be a grafter
You knew it wouldn't be too easy
In that great big world out there to find
A career that would give you most security
And to live your life with peace of mind
But if you were asked to look back, in life
Is there something you would choose to change
Or do you merely accept life as it is
And nothing wish to re-arrange
For life is a long and winding road
And wisdom comes with age
Instead of growing older, as you think
In your book of life you've written another page
And now you've come back to the present day
Is there somewhere you'd like to go
Or are you content to sit in the Garden
And listen to your Radio.

Dennis Shrubshall   13th July 2009

285